DATE DUE

Wallace
Stevens

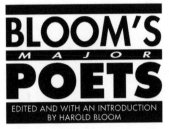

EDITED AND WITH AN INTRODUCTION
BY HAROLD BLOOM

Wallace Stevens

CHELSEA HOUSE
P U B L I S H E R S
A Haights Cross Communications Company
Philadelphia

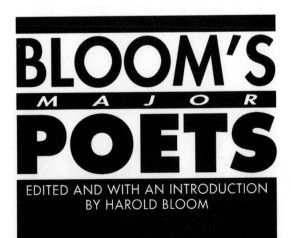

BLOOM'S

MAJOR

POETS

EDITED AND WITH AN INTRODUCTION
BY HAROLD BLOOM

© 2003 by Chelsea House Publishers, a subsidiary of
Haights Cross Communications.

A Haights Cross Communications ⚓ Company

Introduction © 2003 by Harold Bloom.

Printed and bound in the United States of America.

First Printing
1 3 5 7 9 8 6 4 2

Library of Congress Cataloging-in-Publication Data

Wallace Stevens / edited and with introduction by Harold Bloom.
     p. cm. — (Bloom's major poets)
Includes bibliographical references and index.
  ISBN 0-7910-7389-0
  1. Stevens, Wallace, 1879–1955—Criticism and interpretation. I.
Bloom, Harold. II. Series.
  PS3537.T4753 Z87 2002
  811'.52—dc21

                             2002151352

Chelsea House Publishers
1974 Sproul Road, Suite 400
Broomall, PA 19008-0914
http://www.chelseahouse.com

Contributing Editor: Gabriel Welsch

Cover design by Keith Trego

Layout by EJB Publishing Services

CONTENTS

USER'S GUIDE

This volume is designed to present biographical, critical, and bibliographical information on the author and the author's best-known or most important poems. Following Harold Bloom's editor's note and introduction is a concise biography of the author that discusses major life events and important literary accomplishments. A critical analysis of each poem follows, tracing significant themes, patterns, and motifs in the work. As with any study guide, it is recommended that the reader read the poem beforehand, and have a copy of the poem being discussed available for quick reference.

A selection of critical extracts, derived from previously published material, follows each thematic analysis. In most cases, these extracts represent the best analysis available from a number of leading critics. Because these extracts are derived from previously published material, they will include the original notations and references when available. Each extract is cited, and readers are encouraged to check the original publication as they continue their research. A bibliography of the author's writings, a list of additional books and articles on the author and their work, and an index of themes and ideas conclude the volume.

ABOUT THE EDITOR

Harold Bloom is Sterling Professor of the Humanities at Yale University and Henry W. and Albert A. Berg Professor of English at the New York University Graduate School. He is the author of over 20 books, and the editor of more than 30 anthologies of literary criticism.

Professor Bloom's works include *Shelley's Mythmaking* (1959), *The Visionary Company* (1961), *Blake's Apocalypse* (1963), *Yeats* (1970), *A Map of Misreading* (1975), *Kabbalah and Criticism* (1975), *Agon: Toward a Theory of Revisionism* (1982), *The American Religion* (1992), *The Western Canon* (1994), and *Omens of Millennium: The Gnosis of Angels, Dreams, and Resurrection* (1996). *The Anxiety of Influence* (1973) sets forth Professor Bloom's provocative theory of the literary relationships between the great writers and their predecessors. His most recent books include *Shakespeare: The Invention of the Human*, a 1998 National Book Award finalist, *How to Read and Why* (2000), and *Genius: A Mosaic of One Hundred Exemplary Creative Minds* (2002).

Professor Bloom earned his Ph.D. from Yale University in 1955 and has served on the Yale faculty since then. He is a 1985 MacArthur Foundation Award recipient and served as the Charles Eliot Norton Professor of Poetry at Harvard University in 1987–88. In 1999 he was awarded the prestigious American Academy of Arts and Letters Gold Medal for Criticism. Professor Bloom is the editor of several other Chelsea House series in literary criticism, including BLOOM'S MAJOR SHORT STORY WRITERS, BLOOM'S MAJOR NOVELISTS, BLOOM'S MAJOR DRAMATISTS, BLOOM'S MODERN CRITICAL INTERPRETATIONS, BLOOM'S MODERN CRITICAL VIEWS, and BLOOM'S BIOCRITIQUES.

EDITOR'S NOTE

My Introduction offers an appreciation of Wallace Stevens's great crisis-poem, "The Auroras of Autumn."

"Sunday Morning" receives six studies, of which I particularly commend that of J. Hillis Miller on Stevens's imagistic eloquence.

"The Idea of Order at Key West" is illuminated particularly by B.J. Leggett on Nietzschean perspectivism in the poem.

Of the six critical views on "Notes Toward a Supreme Fiction," all are supremely useful.

On "The Auroras of Autumn," the brilliant commentary by Charles Berger is supplemented interestingly by that of Joseph G. Kronick.

Charles Berger returns elucidating "The Course of a Particular," while George S. Lensing takes the poem full-circle back to "The Snow Man."

INTRODUCTION
Harold Bloom

Since I find myself in what William Butler Yeats called "the Autumn of the Body," I write this Introduction as a conscious farewell to the poet who formed my mind, as I am not likely ever to find occasion to meditate again in print upon him.

I will confine these remarks to what may be Stevens's masterwork, the magnificent *The Auroras of Autumn*, composed when Stevens was sixty-eight in 1947. One could argue that *Notes Toward A Supreme Fiction* (1942) is Stevens's formal attempt at his major poem, and I have moods when I favor *An Ordinary Evening in New Haven* (1949). And yet, on balance, *The Auroras of Autumn*, is Stevens' version of the American Sublime, a worthy companion to the Walt Whitman of the great elegies: "Out of the Cradle Endlessly Rocking," "As Ebb'd with the Ocean of Life," and "When Lilacs Last in the Dooryard Bloom'd."

I have been teaching, and writing about, *The Auroras of Autumn* for nearly a half-century, and will not attempt a comprehensive commentary here, like the rather elaborate one offered in my book, *Wallace Stevens: The Poems of our Climate* (1977). Walter Pater called a superb volume of critical essays, *Appreciations*, and in my old age increasingly I want to write "Appreciations" of the great works of imaginative literature.

The Auroras of Autumn, at first, can seem a rather difficult poem, though after so many decades of possessing it by memory, the complexities smooth out, and something like a total coherence prevails. My students generally find Canto I of the poem the most immediately hard to absorb, particularly the now famous three opening tercets:

> This is where the serpent lives, the bodiless.
> His head is air. Beneath his tip at night
> Eyes open and fix on us in every sky.
>
> Or is this another wriggling out of the egg,
> Another image at the end of the cave,
> Another bodiless for the body's slough?

> This is where the serpent lives. This is his nest,
> These fields, these hills, these tinted distances,
> And the pines above and along and beside the sea.

Stevens, in this most personal and dramatic of all his poems, sets the scene carefully, but obliquely. An extraordinary conflagration of the aurora borealis or Northern Lights bursts above him in the evening sky, even as summer yields to autumn. Looking up, the aging poet beholds the auroras lashing across the heavens like a giant serpent extending and then withdrawing. He walks the beach, with fields, hills, pines behind him, while (implicitly) he alternately surveys sky, sea, and land. Since the illumination of the auroras is pervasive, the entire scene is the serpent's nest, while the eyes opening beneath the serpent's tip are the stars, captive to the aurora—serpent's reign. Yet, in the second tercet the poet allows himself a momentary skepticism: are the great lights only another mythic origin (wriggling out of the egg), or another illusion on the wall of Plato's cave, or a wish-fulfillment of an old man heavily caught in the body's slough, and identifying with the serpent's bodilessness?

Cantos II-IV of *The Auroras of Autumn* all begin with the phrase: "Farewell to an idea." Stevens relies upon the reader's knowledge of *Notes Toward a Supreme Fiction*, where "the first idea" or snow man's reality is perpetually reimagined. It is the idea of reimagining the first idea to which the poet now says farewell. Canto II is so brilliant that I need to appreciate it very closely here:

> Farewell to an idea.... A cabin stands,
> Deserted, on a beach. It is white,
> As by a custom or according to
>
> An ancestral theme or as a consequence
> Of an infinite course. The flowers against the wall
> Are white, a little dried, a kind of mark
>
> Reminding, trying to remind, of a white
> That was different, something else, last year
> Or before, not the white of an aging afternoon,
>
> Whether fresher or duller, whether of winter cloud
> Or of winter sky, from horizon to horizon.
> The wind is blowing the sand across the floor.

Here, being visible is being white,
Is being of the solid of white, the accomplishment
Of an extremist in an exercise...

The season changes. A cold wind chills the beach.
The long lines of it grow longer, emptier,
A darkness gathers though it does not fall

And the whiteness grows less vivid on the wall.
The man who is walking turns blankly on the sand.
He observes how the north is always enlarging the change,

With its frigid brilliances, its blue-red sweeps
Ands gusts of great enkindlings, its polar green,
The color of ice and fire and solitude.

A great and frightening, metaphorical tradition of the "blank" culminates as Stevens walks the beach: "The man who is walking turns *blankly* on the sand" (my italics). John Milton, blindly invoking the Holy Light, laments "a universal blank/of Nature's works to me expunged and razed." Samuel Taylor Coleridge, confronting his Dejection, stares upon a foreboding sky: "And still I gaze-and with how blank an eye!" Coleridge alludes to Milton, and Ralph Waldo Emerson, in his *Nature*, subsumes them both: "The ruin or blank that we see when we look at nature is in our own eye." Emily Dickinson, obsessed with the metaphor of the blank, sees herself as going: "From Blank to Blank," in a labyrinth without a guiding thread. In Stevens, the sinister white of his reductions to a first idea modulates into a blank that his own imagination has created. The man who is walking the sands, the sixty-eight year old poet, turns blankly, because he observes a blank, with an eye that is blank, in the context of a universal blank, while knowing that all the poems he has composed now seem blank. The Northern Lights enlarge the change, confronting him with ruin.

A strong poet, Stevens fights back against the auroras in Canto III and IV, summoning up the images of his late mother and father. But memory dissolves in the glare of the Northern Lights:

And yet she too is dissolved, she is destroyed.
She gives transparences. But she has grown old.
The necklace is a carving not a kiss.

The soft hands are a motion not a touch.

It is at the close of Canto VI that Stevens achieves the apotheosis of this crisis poem. A lifetime of imaginative discipline courageously attempts to unname the auroras, but is defeated by the uncanny terror brought about by the responsive flaming-up of the Northern Lights:

This is nothing until in a single man contained,
Nothing until this named thing nameless is
And is destroyed. He opens the doors of his house

On flames. The scholar of one candle sees
An Arctic effulgence flaring on the frame
Of everything he is. And he feels afraid.

The scholar is Emerson's "Man thinking," but thought cannot prevail when the house of the spirit opens its door on the flames of the auroras. Subtly, Stevens works through his dilemmas until in Canto VIII, he can affirm the innocence of the auroras:

So, then, these lights are not a spell of light,
A saying out of a cloud, but innocence.
An innocence of the earth and no false sign

Or symbol of malice.

It is, from Hamlet through Milton on to the High Romantics and Wallace Stevens, the poetic enterprise proper to affirm the power of the mind over a universe of death. In *The Auroras of Autumn*, Stevens paradoxically experiences the defeat of that enterprise, and yet continues it even in apparent defeat. If the Sublime poem exists in twentieth century American English, *The Auroras of Autumn*, in my judgement, joins Hart Crane's *The Bridge* as one of its leading exemplars.

BIOGRAPHY OF

Wallace Stevens

A mythology persists in surrounding Wallace Stevens, despite the best efforts of critics and enthusiasts of his work to reveal the supreme *non*fiction about the man as his canonical stock has risen in the last few decades. To those who have heard of him in passing, he is often characterized as an aesthete, as one withdrawn from the major artistic and social movements of the first half of the twentieth century. If the casual reader knows anything about him, it is most likely to be that he walked to and from work (mostly true), that his co-workers at Hartford Accident and Indemnity had no idea he was a poet, so assiduously did he keep it from them (utterly false), and that he was a prudish, mildly priggish man who would rather scribble than do much else (gross oversimplification).

Wallace Stevens was born in Reading, Pennsylvania, on October 2, 1879. He was the second of four children, and the only one not given a family name. Thus, on the very occasion of his birth, he was marked in one small way (which loomed in his imagination later) as being one on the outside. He competed with his brothers in the private school to which their father, Garrett, an artistically-inclined though financially pragmatic lawyer, sent them. While attending the school, young Wallace distinguished himself as an orator and a writer, early moves to call attention to his mind and not his size. He grew into a great man by the standards of the day, and was self-conscious about his bulk, even though others admired his strength. As an adult, his crisp and economical movements arose from a lifetime of suppressing his physical presence.

The suppression might also explain why Stevens was so enamored of walking. The habit began in Reading, as an adolescent. Awkward with girls and impatient in the company of most boys, Stevens often took long walks for solitude, thought, and observation. Often the walks were fifteen or twenty miles or more. Because of the joy he derived from his strolls, the habit persisted into adulthood. For most of his adult life, he walked the several miles to and from his Hartford offices most every day. The years of walking provided Stevens the images of his work, the grist for the philosophic and abstract notions that moved him on his perambulations, and which resonated throughout his existence. He once referred to the thoughts that came to him on those walks, in his solitude, as the only "real life" he had.

In 1897, Stevens left Reading to attend Harvard College, and while he never fully earned a degree from the institution, it was a critical development in his intellectual life. During his time there, he read a great deal of Latin and Greek; studied the ideas of Charles Darwin, Arthur Schopenhauer, Sigmund Freud, Karl Marx; digested Whitman and the Romantic poets; and met contacts that would provide him a network and entrée to work in New York. While at Harvard, he wrote for and, for a short time, edited the *Advocate*. Often as editor, he would publish work he wrote under pseudonym to provide sufficient material to fill the pages. The fact that he did so reveals how little he found to inspire him in the literary community at Cambridge.

When Stevens left Harvard in 1900, New York offered scarcely more in terms of a literary community. Mostly, Stevens lamented the common and the dirty so prevalent in the city at the time. He may have done so because of the particulars of his exposure to it. He worked as a journalist, trolling Manhattan for stories for the *New York Evening Post*. Whenever he could, he would return to Reading to reinvigorate his spirit on the wooded trails and among the fields that were growing increasingly sacred to him while he lived in New York. While his relationship to his family and the religious provincialism of his hometown grew more complicated and he found himself increasingly alienated from them, his value of and yearning for the landscape itself grew more profound. Nonetheless, by the end of 1901, when he finally tired of journalism and followed his father's "practical" nature and advice and enrolled in the New York School of Law, he considered himself practically severed from his home and his relations.

In 1904, he was admitted to the New York Bar and took his first position as a law clerk for a former Harvard contact. He worked for a number of firms over the next few years before taking a position at the American Bonding Company in 1908 (the company was later purchased and became Fidelity and Deposit Company). During those years, he absorbed what he could of New York's cultural life, attending musicals and theatre productions, writing plays himself that he hoped to see staged. At the same time, his trips to Reading brought him into contact with Elsie Viola Kechel, known as Elsie Moll, an incorrect name but a term of convenience as Elsie's family history was jumbled and her childhood was spent, in Stevens' terms, "on the wrong side of the tracks."

Stevens was introduced to Elsie as a poet from New York, and was thus treated as a worldly and accomplished man. Joan Richardson has pointed out that Stevens' older bearing (he was 27 when he met Elsie, and she was 19) and the promise of affluence was a powerful motivation for Elsie to return his affections, despite what appeared to be an initial ambivalence. Several biographers have commented on Elsie's lack of sophistication. Some have suggested that her intellectual position relative to Stevens' was a good match to his emotional immaturity. As well, Elsie was considered a strikingly beautiful woman. (In fact, in 1913, the couple lived in an apartment above the studio of sculptor Adolph A. Weinmann, who asked Elsie to pose for a bust-model for his famous (among numismatists) 1916 Liberty Head dime.) Whatever the attraction, the two married in 1909, just as Stevens' insurance law career was gaining momentum. By most accounts, the marriage, though long-lasting, was not satisfying. Elsie spent summers, for the most part, in Reading or in the Poconos, leaving Stevens at home to juggle routine household details and the management of his penchants for indulgence in food, drink, and cigars. They did have a daughter, Holly Bright Stevens, born in 1924, who went on to be an important editor of Stevens' posthumous publications, as well as his letters, but the intellectual and emotional differences in the two became extremely apparent after they began to live together. Because their courtship was one predominantly occurring in letters, most of which written by Stevens and modeling a romanticized future (as well as romanticized lovers), the resulting reality of the day-to-day facts of their marriage—Stevens' seldom keeping her company in the evenings, preferring books or long walks, Elsie's feeling isolated and restricted in the worlds of New York and Hartford— aggravated a distance that grew between them over the years.

By 1912, both of Stevens' parents had died, roughly within a year of one another. As his visits to Reading became far less frequent, Stevens was writing regularly and prolifically the poems that would become *Harmonium*. In 1913 he took a position with the Equitable Surety Company as resident vice-president. At the same time, he was beginning to send work to editors, and to develop tastes in artwork, particularly in contemporary Asian art. He pursued friendships with people involved in the art world, and began to collect pieces. He befriended Walter Arenberg and Walter Pach, met and associated with Marcel Duchamp, and cultivated an enthusiastic appreciation of the newest artists, all associated with the Armory Show of 1913. While he generally avoided the literary world present in New York at the time, he did begin friendships with the writers William Carlos Williams and Marianne Moore, which would last for decades. Equitable Surety transferred Stevens to their Hartford office, and by 1916, two years after his poems began appearing in major journals, including four poems which appeared in a special "War Poems" issue of Harriet Monroe's *Poetry*, Stevens made his final career change. He joined Hartford Accident and Indemnity Corporation, where he remained until his retirement from insurance.

For the next several years, Stevens produced and published a number of his most important poems. He would not publish *Harmonium* until 1923, and in the meantime he won an award for one of his plays, as well as *Poetry's* Levinson Prize in 1920. At the same time, he grew increasingly accomplished in his insurance career, and grew to feel that poetry was completing the life he was living, in ways that both marriage and a professional career had not. Thus, while he was still a very obscure poet, by the time *Harmonium* appeared, those who followed and wrote poetry were not unfamiliar with his work.

Harmonium had a mixed reception. Harriet Monroe reviewed it favorably, but the *New York Times* was dismissive, claiming the book's aesthetic was dated, and calling Stevens (even after the expanded re-issue of *Harmonium* in 1931), "a martyr for a lost cause." Most other reviewers landed somewhere in between in their enthusiasm for the book. To Stevens, however, the critics mattered little. After *Harmonium* appeared, Stevens wrote very little for a time. Stevens' own claims are that he did not write for six years, but there is evidence he thought of poetry as early as 1927. Naturally, with a newborn in the house and a growing slate of responsibilities at home, Stevens' rhythms changed. With Holly added to the house, his business travel taking him away from his home and study more and more often, the time which Stevens could devote to writing dwindled. He also renewed his efforts at work, stating in one letter that he had much he wanted to do, that he hated the idea of poverty, and so devoted himself to work.

Critics see the poems that eventually did result, and which would comprise 1935's *Ideas of Order*, published by Alcestis Press, and later, in an enlarged edition by Knopf in 1936, as lacking the cynicism and abrasive humor of Stevens' debut. While Stevens has written little to nothing on how the birth of his daughter affected him, some have pointed to Holly's arrival as an agent that took the edge off Stevens' view of the world, and also eased his own self-censure. *Ideas of Order* was well received; however, *Owl's Clover*, a prose meditation on poetry as an art form, was not.

Stevens' reputation was not fully solidified until after the next three Knopf releases: *The Man with the Blue Guitar, and Other Poems* in 1937, *Parts of a World*, in 1942, and *Transport to Summer* in 1947, the final volume containing such famous and important poems as "Esthétique du Mal" and "Notes Toward A Supreme Fiction." During that time his friendships with Marianne Moore and William Carlos Williams deepened, and in the case of the latter, complicated. (While Stevens wrote an introduction for Williams' *Collected Poems 1921–1931*, the two poets differed, sometimes harshly, on poetic matters.) As well, his hard work of the years after Holly's birth had paid off; Stevens was promoted to a vice-president position at the Hartford Accident and Insurance Company.

He had also succeeded, by those years, to order his life so that he could efficiently manage the demands he made of himself and his art. While meeting the rigors of a complicated home-life and the raising of his daughter, he also made peace with the writing process such that the thirties and forties were, for Stevens, the most constant and prolific time of his life. He was also asked to lecture at universities and arts centers, to write on the subject of poetry, and to in all ways behave as an elder of the craft.

In 1950, those years of effort paid off as well. He had already won a few awards, including the *Nation's* poetry award in 1936, and the Harriet Monroe Award from *Poetry* in 1946, but following the publication of *The Auroras of Autumn* by Knopf in 1950, Stevens was awarded the National Book Award, the Bollingen Prize from Yale University, and the Poetry Society of America's Gold Medal in 1951. Then, three years later, following publication of *The Collected Poems of Wallace Stevens* by Knopf in 1954, Stevens won the National Book Award again, the first person ever to have won the award twice. He won the Pulitzer Prize the following year. As well, Bard College, Mount Holyoke, Columbia, Harvard, and Yale all awarded Stevens honorary degrees in the fifties.

By the time he died, on August 2, 1954, after being in a coma for two days, he had secured a position, while still alive, as a preeminent person in American letters. Conflating, as he once stated, the "world of Plato ... [and] the world of Darwin" into a body of work both comic and prescient, specific and abstract, Wallace Stevens elucidated the path toward the supreme fiction, broke American poetry tradition from the Romantics as well as from the arrogant extremes of twentieth century modishness. A concerned political poet (as his letters reveal), a passionate enthusiast of the arts and the history of his country and its landscape, and a rigorous businessperson, Stevens embodied some of the best of the twentieth century in making its transition from the centuries before.

CRITICAL ANALYSIS OF

"Sunday Morning"

Published in Harriet Monroe's *Poetry* in 1915 and later collected in the 1923 collection, *Harmonium*, "Sunday Morning" is regarded by many Stevens' critics to be his first important poem, and a prelude to the philosophical concerns and segmented structures that would characterize the better-known poems of his later years. In eight regular stanza sections of fifteen lines apiece—which, like the sonnet form they so resemble, contain a hinge upon which the reasoning within each section turns—Stevens sets forth his first "serious" poem on religious and philosophical matters, contrasting in content (if not entirely in style) against the comic and meditative works more typical of his first collection, which included "Le Monocle de Mon Oncle," "The Comedian as Letter C," and "Thirteen Ways of Looking at a Blackbird."

"Sunday Morning" is essentially a meditation upon a meditation. The first stanza sets the scene, and a contrast, as a number of critics have shown, between the physical and the spiritual. The first word is, crucially, "Complacencies." It is quickly revealed as a description of the peignoir, but it nonetheless sets the tone of the woman being considered here. Due to her relative comfort—the oranges, the rug with the cockatoo motif, the sunny chair and the "late coffee,"—she is a manifestation of early twentieth-century affluence, or at least emerging middle-class comfort. In that comfort, that complacency or lack of urgency due to her presumed station in society, she is able to muse, to "dream a little" on religious matters. So genteel are her environs that even the bloody Crucifixion becomes, in Stevens' treatment, "the holy hush of ancient sacrifice." Her comfort serves "to dissipate" the reverence of a Sunday, just as for the poet, the woods and rivers of Reading would often dissipate the starchy formality and removal of his family's own stringent religious observations. It is worth noting that the poem was written three years after the death of his mother, the main religious force in his life, and who was the root of Stevens' spiritual education. While he had certainly been stewing about his distaste for being a good Puritan for some time, he did not approach it forcefully and ironically until after his mother's death.

As the woman dreams of that "old catastrophe," and Stevens' verse places the defining moment of Christian faith as a relic, all is still around her. The world calms—"a calm darkens among water-lights"—and she is away, "Over the seas, to silent Palestine, / Dominion of the blood and sepulchre." His words at the stanza's end imbue the scene of the burial with more *gravitas*, as the site itself becomes important in later stanzas. In this poem, the site and its physical characteristics, and the fact that it contains the death, are more important than the miracle Christians believe followed.

The second stanza, as Robert Rehder points out (see below), contains the questions that are the grist of the meditation. "Why should she give her bounty to the dead? / What is divinity if it can come / Only in silent shadows and in dreams? / Shall she not find comforts of the sun / In ... things to be cherished like the thought of heaven?" The questions place the understanding, and therefore creation, by Stevens' philosophy, of heaven firmly within her mind. Thus, the divine is an agent, creation, and projection of the self. This is a major theme of Stevens' and is approached with ever-greater abstraction and precision through the rest of his writing.

Once the questions are posed in the stanza, the poem states, "Divinity must live within herself:" The examples that follow and make specific the statement reveal what sort of divinity Stevens envisions. The examples are sensual aspects of the seasons, feelings and perceptions and not objects or things. The assertion that divinity is both within a person and comprised of the sensations that are remembered is not a conclusion the woman draws herself; rather, the poetic persona makes it, rendering the poem a meditation articulating what the character in the poem cannot. The "psychic distance" (to use a term from fiction writer John Gardner) of this narrator from the material at hand is necessary for the following stanza, which speculates on the genesis of God.

Note, however, that Stevens does not say God. It is possible there remains a bit of the Puritan in him, still, at this point (and his biographers bear this out). He instead talks of Jove, and in gentle blasphemy points out that the deity is without a mother, but more importantly, without a land to give "Large-mannered motions to his mythy mind." For Stevens, religion and mythology arose from landscape, an idea very important to him and expressed most directly in another poem, written late in life and collected in *Opus Posthumous*, "A Mythology Reflects Its Region." Thus, without the land to "make" him, Jove "moved among us, as a muttering king" to his "hinds," an archaic term for peasants, with the bawdy overtones of hindquarters, or of deer. The "commingling" of "Our blood" resonates from the myths of the Greek gods (and here Jove, Zeus, and God are conflated), and it is clear Stevens is making reference to the conception of Christ, an event of such magnitude that "The very hinds discerned it, in a star." But the stanza turns right afterward when the poet asks, "Shall our blood fail? Or shall it come to be / The blood of paradise? And shall the earth / Seem all of paradise that we shall know?" The inference is that the dead will stay in the ground, not ascend, but become part of the terrestrial paradise, part of that system of seasons and sensations from which we extrapolate an imagined paradise, a divinity that has its genesis in us. The heavens, then, are characterized, finally, as a "dividing and indifferent blue."

The fourth stanza has the woman expressing her comfort, again—though this time in her words—at the advent of birds. The moment, we see, is her paradise, for she asks where paradise is once the birds alight. The poet answers: religion is neither the means toward nor the Platonic shadow of paradise. No "old chimera of the grave," making the Christ myth into a monster of many parts. He further points out that nothing of the physical environment, including the birds, or the "cloudy palm" will endure or outlast memory's pictures of earthly paradises. Nothing lasts as does the imagination of heaven, and thus only the imagination of heaven is paradise.

As if answering the poet in the next stanza, the woman expresses her need "of some imperishable bliss," in addition to the momentary, and thus perishable, bliss of seeing the bird. Stevens answers with another important and aphoristic moment in the poem: "Death is the mother of beauty; hence, from her, / Alone, shall come fulfillment to our dreams/ And our desires." Death is the process from which and toward which all sensation moves. The sensation, that which causes the dreams and wistful imaginings of both the boys and maidens evoked in the stanzas (and the archetypes of Romantic poetry they embody, and at which Stevens here is poking gentle fun), is key to paganism, which, after all, is what Stevens proclaimed the poem to be about in his letters.

The next two stanzas depart from the to and fro quality of the meditation to this point in the poem. Stanza VI questions the conventional imagination of paradise, asking "Is there no change of death in paradise?/ Does ripe fruit never fall?" Such a vision of paradise, one seen without the passage of time, becomes one of "insipid" stasis. Without the drama of change, paradise would be something else. Thus, again, Stevens repeats "Death is the mother of beauty, mystical, / Within whose burning bosom we devise / Our earthly mothers waiting, sleeplessly." The aspects of waiting and sleeplessness, contrasted with the static idea of death, indicate a process that allows for the imagination of paradise. The waiting and the yearning, the opposite of complacency, are what allow for paradise to be imagined, when one takes enjoyment, life (hence mothers are imagined here), from the sensations of one's surroundings.

The following stanza imagines the bawdy scene of an orgy of chanting men, "Supple and turbulent," in marked contrast, again, to the complacency of the poem's opening. They are chanting to the sun (an important entity in Stevens, and a conceit within "Notes Toward A Supreme Fiction", *q.v.*), and in their actions they are "as a god might be." The god, in Stevens' reasoning, would be this sensual, this corporeal, this exultant, since paradise is so fleeting. Indeed, "Their chant shall be a chant of paradise," and the very place where they are is transformed through repetition of Biblical imagery into a sacred space. In fact, the scene's evocation of serafin echoes Isaiah's vision of the throne of God, and here the poet imagines what a god would do in the scene. The trees are likened to angels, the hills are a choir, and their journey, their fleeting attainment of paradise will only be in heavenly fellowship, the shared knowledge of their mortality and that the life they live here is the only life they will have. No afterlife, no paradise beyond this. All they will have of their journey is "the dew upon their feet," which doubtless will dry.

In the final stanza, the woman hears an answer from where her "dreaming feet" have gone: the tomb of Jesus is only "where he lay." It is not sacred; it is not of heaven. The statement implies that he is still there, mortal as the rest of us, as the men in the orgy for the sun. His spirit has gone nowhere. Instead, "We live in an old chaos of the sun, / Or old dependency on day and night / Or island solitude, unsponsored, free, / Of that wide water, inescapable." The natural details of the ending lines are reaffirming the source of paradise: earthly environs, their change, the constancy of death. When the pigeons themselves are mentioned, they embody the noble tragedy of our journey. They make paradise while being cognizant of what awaits: "casual flocks of pigeons make / Ambiguous undulations as they sink, / Downward to darkness, on extended wings."

CRITICAL VIEWS ON

"Sunday Morning"

J. HILLIS MILLER ON THE ELOQUENCE OF THE POEM'S MENTAL FICTION

[Since 1986, J. Hillis Miller has held the title of Distinguished Professor of English and Comparative Literature at the University of California, Irvine. Among his numerous honors, Miller recently was named Honorary Professor of Shandong University, and Honorary Professor of Peking University, both in the People's Republic of China. His most recent books include *Others* (forthcoming from Princeton UP), *Speech Acts in Literature* (forthcoming from Stanford UP), and, *Black Holes*, his part of a double book written in collaboration with Manuel Asensi (Stanford, 1999). In the excerpt, Miller discusses Stevens' portrayal of the strength of humanity in the face of a world where the gods have, in Miller's words, "dissolved." Miller links Stevens' later prose writings, collected primarily in *Opus Posthumous*, to the ideas in "Sunday Morning."]

"Sunday Morning" is Stevens' most eloquent description of the moment when the gods dissolve. Bereft of the supernatural, man does not lie down paralyzed in despair. He sings the creative hymns of a new culture, the culture of those who are "wholly human" and know themselves (*CP*, 317). This humanism is based on man's knowledge that "the final belief is to believe in a fiction, which you know to be a fiction, there being nothing else. The exquisite truth is to know that it is a fiction and that you believe in it willingly" (*OP*, 163). There is "nothing else"—the alternatives are to be nothing or to accept a fiction. To discover that there never has been any celestial world is a joyful liberation, and man says of himself: "This happy creature—It is he that invented the Gods. It is he that put into their mouths the only words they have ever spoken!" (*OP*, 167).

To discover that man has invented the gods is to find out the dependence of the mind on nature. Mental fictions are derived from material things: "All of our ideas come from the natural world: trees = umbrellas" (*OP*, 163). Since this is true, the only way to give mental fictions authenticity is to base them on the world of sun and rain and April: "The real is only the base. But it is the base" (*OP*, 160). When Stevens speaks this way, he is a poet of a happy naturalism. In many eloquent passages he celebrates the joy of "the latest freed man" (*CP*, 204), the man who has escaped from the gods and is able to step barefoot into reality. This man has shed the old myths as a snake sheds its skin, and can cry in exultation: "the past is dead. / Her mind will never speak to me again. / I am free" (*CP*, 117). Liberated from the bad faith which attributed to some never-never land the glory of earth, man does not lose the golden glory of heaven. He transfers to what is close and real, the "in-bar," what he had falsely ascribed to transcendent realms, the "ex-bar" (*CP*, 317). Culture has always been based on the permanences of sun, air, and earth. Now man knows that this is so. He knows that "The greatest poverty is not to live / In a physical world" (*CP*, 325), and this brings about a sudden miraculous recovery, of the vitality of earth.

But umbrellas are not trees. Even the nakedest man is not part of nature in the same way that stones or trees are. Man possesses imagination, and, though "the imagination is one of the forces of nature" (*OP*, 170), the peculiar potency of this force is to transform nature, to make trees into umbrellas. In changing nature, the imagination irradiates it with its own idiosyncratic hue. The poet must accept this distortion as in the nature of things. The green of reality is altered by the blue of imagination, and there is no helping this fact. The mind turns to reality and is enriched by it, but it also shapes the real into myths, religions, and other forms of poetry. The worst evil is a victory of one power over the other, a romanticism which kicks itself loose of the earth, or a pressure of reality so great that it overwhelms imagination. "Eventually an imaginary world is entirely without interest" (*OP*, 175), but, on the other hand, man today is confronting events "beyond [his] power to reduce them and metamorphose them" (*NA*, 22), and as a result "There are no shadows anywhere. / The earth, for us, is flat and bare" (*CP*, 167). Fresh fictions must now replace the old. The creation, after the death of the gods, of new fictions, based on fact and not pretending to be more than fictions, is the act of poetry. "After one has abandoned a belief in God, poetry is that essence which takes its place as life's redemption" (*OP*, 158). In defining poetry as a substitute for religion Stevens is joining himself to a tradition extending from the romantics through Matthew Arnold down to our own day.

The dialogue between subject and object is Stevens' central theme, and it seems that this interchange can become a "mystic marriage," like that of the great captain and the maiden Bawda in "Notes Toward a Supreme Fiction" (*CP*, 401). Imagination and reality can merge to produce a third thing which escapes from the limitations of either, and we can triumphantly "mate [our] life with life" (*CP*, 222). "If it should be true that reality exists / In the mind ... it follows that / Real and unreal are two in one" (*CP*, 485). The red of reality and the blue of imagination join to become the "purple tabulae" on which may be read the poem of life (*CP*, 424). It is not necessary to choose between Don Quixote and Sancho Panza. Man can have both, and poetry is the search for those fortuitous conjunctions between self and world which show that they are not irreconcilable opposites, but two sides of the same coin, "equal and inseparable" (*NA*, 24).

The poverty following the death of the gods can apparently be transcended without difficulty. Stevens' real choice is neither for the subjectivism coming down from Descartes nor for the submission to physical nature which he sometimes praises. His tradition is rather perspectivism, historicism, *lebensphilosophie*. He is one of the subtlest expositors of this tradition. His predecessors are Feuerbach, Dilthey, Nietzsche, Ortega y Gasset, Santayana, and Henri Focillon, the Focillon whose *Vie des formes* Stevens calls "one of the really remarkable books of the day" (*NA*, 46). Like these thinkers, Stevens sees human history as the constant proliferation of forms of art and culture which are valid only for one time and place. These are determined exclusively neither by geography nor by the untrammeled human mind, but everywhere are the offspring of a marriage of man and the place where he lives. The fact that one man's fictions can be accepted by others makes society possible. "An age is a manner collected from a queen. / An age is green or red. An age believes / Or it denies," and "Things are as they seemed to Calvin or to Anne / Of England, to Pablo Neruda in Ceylon, / To Nietzsche in Basel, to Lenin by a Lake" (*CP*, 340, 341, 342).

In human history two things are constantly happening. Men are always being bent to their environment, driven to make their life forms a mirror of the weather of their place, for "the gods grow out of the weather. / The people grow out of the weather" (*CP*, 210), and "the natives of the rain are rainy men" (*CP*, 37). On the other hand, the mind organizes the land in which it finds itself, as the moon makes concentric circles in the random twigs of a leafless tree, or as the jar in Tennessee orders the wilderness around it and takes dominion every where. The jar is a human artifact. Its man-made shape has the power to structure everything radially around it, as the red queen makes a whole age red. The jar is one of the "Imaginary poles whose intelligence / Stream[s] over chaos their civilities" (*CP*, 479).

Stevens' work can be summed up in two adages: "The soul ... is composed / Of the external world" (*CP*, 51); "It is never the thing but the version of the thing" (*CP*, 332). His poetry is the reconciliation of these two truths, truths which are always simultaneously binding in the endless intercourse of imagination and reality. Words are the best marriage-place of mind and world. In language a people gives speech to its environment, and at the same time it creates itself in that speech. Language is at once the expression of a style of life and the embodiment of a local weather and geography.

—J. Hillis Miller. "Wallace Stevens." *Critical Essays on Wallace Stevens*, edited by Steven Gould Axelrod and Helen Deese. Boston: G.K. Hall & Co., 1988, pp. 81–83.

ROBERT REHDER ON CHARACTER AND STRUCTURE

[Robert Rehder is Professor of English at the University of Fribourg in Switzerland. A poet and critic, Rehder is the author of *Wordsworth and the Beginnings of Modern Poetry* and *The Poetry of Wallace Stevens*, as well as a collection of poems, *The Compromises Will Be Different*. Rehder discusses the character of the woman and the character of Stevens' voice at the outset of the poem, making comparisons to Wordsworth while also noting the implicit contract Stevens makes with the reader of the poem.]

There is one poem in *Harmonium* that by its seriousness stands out in the same way as 'Lines Written a Few Miles above Tintern Abbey' stands out in *Lyrical Ballads*. This is 'Sunday Morning', the first great poem that Stevens wrote and probably his best-known work, offering a definition of genius in that it seems to come almost from nowhere. None of his previous poems have exactly this tone or are anything like as good. 'Sunday Morning' can be said to inaugurate Stevens' first period of major work (1915–24). Here, all at once, the poet is in full possession of his powers. The poem consists of eight 15-line stanzas in blank verse of a power unmatched by any English poet since Wordsworth, except Browning.

The poem represents the thoughts attributed by the poet to a woman who sits comfortably over a late breakfast on a Sunday morning musing upon the Crucifixion. Although her emotions upon this occasion become clear to us, she remains a shadowy figure without either a personality or a history—Stevens' way of keeping the thoughts at a remove from himself without handing them over to anyone else, and a sign that he sees them as somehow feminine. The woman appears to have just got up, and in her 'sunny chair' 'She dreams a little'. The poem is a daydream, a meditation on the near edge of sleep that emerges from a darkening calm:

> I
> Complacencies of the peignoir, and late
> Coffee and oranges in a sunny chair,
> And the green freedom of a cockatoo
> Upon a rung mingle to dissipate
> The holy hush of ancient sacrifice.
> She dreams a little, and she feels the dark
> Encroachment of that old catastrophe,
> As a calm darkens among water-lights.
> The pungent oranges and bright, green wings
> Seem things in some procession of the dead,
> Winding across wide water, without sound.
> The day is like wide water, without sound,
> Stilled for the passing of her dreaming feet
> Over the seas, to silent Palestine,
> Dominion of the blood and sepulchre.

Where the woman is not specified, only that she is far away in space and time from the scenes of the New Testament story. The death of Jesus, in Stevens' carefully muted references, is an 'ancient sacrifice', 'that old catastrophe', almost suggesting that there might be some temporal limit to belief, although the woman is so pervaded by the story that she thinks of walking on the water to Palestine. Removed from the scene of the action, she feels that in order to understand it she has to go and see for herself. The repetition of 'wide water without sound' in successive lines lulls us into her daydream. Reality is watery here, too. Her thoughts feel like twilight on water, and the day is like a soundless expanse of still water. The major antithesis in the poem is stated in the first sentence: the world when vividly apprehended dissipates any unworldly belief. This is a contrast of moods: comfort *versus* sacrifice, living in the world set against living for another world. Peignoir, coffee, oranges, sun, chair and rug negate metaphysics, or, rather, produce their own ontology. Because the woman lives in considerable comfort, her longings bespeak the limits of the body's pleasures. Her surroundings are described with a deliberate sensuality, a luxury of feeling—

hinting vaguely of the jungle with the tropical oranges and cockatoo. The force of the oranges and cockatoo is increased by repetition; in the second half of the stanza they reappear with emphasis, *pungent* and *bright*, in order to characterise the procession of the dead, which as a result seems to belong more to Yucatan than to Palestine. Thus, they are absorbed into the daydream, 'green freedom' subdued, for the moment, to the 'Dominion of the blood and sepulchre'.

The second stanza opens with three questions that sum up its arguments, and in six of the poem's stanzas the main ideas are similarly set forth in clear, simple sentences. That these sentences are usually questions shows the poet's uncertainty about his answers and that tentativeness is an answer. He is satisfied by the play of possibilities; the willing suspension of belief is for him an act of affirming the nature of the world. The difficulty of 'Sunday Morning' derives from the richness of its nuances and the intrinsic difficulty of its subject, that of making meaning of our lives. The poem exemplifies Stevens' knack for plain statement and his habit of combining summary statement and metaphor. This alternation between preliminary minutiae and supreme fictions is one of the many ways in which he resembles Wordsworth. His capacity to keep the poem going frequently appears to depend on repeatedly collecting his thoughts in an abstract form, and this process appears to generate metaphors and often series of similar or connected metaphors. Abstractions are to Stevens almost like a language within language, the theme from which he derives his variations, Diabelli's waltz to Beethoven. He enjoys the sound of finality, but it is a delight to be savoured as a relish to his scepticism. It tempts him with the possibility of another world. Every absolute, however, is putative, no more than one of many possibilities, and Stevens frequently rehearses them all as if he needs to prove that no form is final. He seeks to come to true conclusions with unfixed forms. This, in itself, is an act of interpretation and one that perhaps can be said to be modelled on the rhetorical figure of paradox (the form of so many of Stevens' summary statements): the attempt to create a form that signifies a range of meanings, the substitution of an activity or process for a finite set of denotations and connotations—an effort to interpret change itself.

II

Why should she give her bounty to the dead?
What is divinity if it can come
Only in silent shadows and in dreams?
Shall she not find in comforts of the sun,
In pungent fruit and bright, green wings, or else
In any balm or beauty of the earth,
Things to be cherished like the thought of heaven?
Divinity must live within herself:
Passions of rain, or moods in falling snow;
Grievings in loneliness, or unsubdued
Elations when the forest blooms; gusty
Emotions on wet roads on autumn nights;
All pleasures and all pains, remembering
The bough of summer and the winter branch.
These are the measures destined for her soul.

The three questions subsume the argument of the entire poem. The final stanza, like the last eight lines of this one, is an answer to the third question, and the poem, in a sense, does not progress beyond this point: the remaining six stanzas are a development of the first two. The poem is, as Stevens says of another poem 'A Thought Revolved'—and thoughts are revolved in his poetry so that they can be seen from all sides. His poems usually develop not as a series of steps towards a destination, but as variations on a theme. They go round and round and over and over their subjects, which is how we respond to the thoughts that deeply trouble us. Stevens knows 'The Pleasures of Merely Circulating', but in the nature of his compulsion to repeat there is something that, despite the playfulness and comedy, convinces us of his profound seriousness. The stanza is commonly the unit of repetition, and in many of the longer poems successive stanzas often perform the same activity. The poems do not merely represent the mind's mulling and churning; they are doing what they are describing—like all art, they *are* thinking.

The woman wonders why she should give what she possesses

to the dead, implying that religion is a tax on her substance and centred on death. To ask 'What is divinity ...?' calls all religion, not Christianity alone, into question and makes it a depersonalised abstraction like 'the thought of heaven'. The woman's questions answer themselves. They reveal her slowly forming conclusion that religion is a fantasy, an act of the mind, and show us her thoughts turning back to her surroundings. Tacitly she acknowledges the need for thoughts that can be cherished. Although religion is rejected, she searches her experience of the world for something to take its place. Divinity is not rejected, but confined to the inner world. *Passions* refers what is experienced in the rain to the suffering of Jesus, and *soul* at the close is another indication that this anti-religion is modelled on Christianity. She wants a secular religion based in transitory things, 'comforts of the sun' and moods. She desires the emotion of religion without the theology, and in the poem the negation of religion produces a freeing and proliferation of feeling of all kinds: passions, moods, grievings, elations, emotions. There is a need to feel deeply and variously, and for feeling to be measured. Certainly the soul in its new mode of belief is to have 'measures'. This appears to mean that every pleasure and pain is to be recognised as corresponding to an event in the world, as each enumerated set of feelings (except 'Grievings in loneliness') is presented as a response to the world and its changing weather. There is a difficulty because the beginning of the sentence is separated from the end by so many juxtaposed elements. The basic sentence is

> Divinity must live within herself:...
> All pleasures and all pains, remembering
> The bough of summer and the winter branch.

What is suggested is that the divine is no more than a sum of human feelings; what is stated is the woman's resolution. The *must* appears to represent her decision to contain her longings for a supernatural realm. Pleasure and pain are to be referred to the changing seasons, bounded by the extremes of summer and winter. Our irreversible lives are to be interpreted in terms of a cycle. 'Remembering' takes place 'within herself'; meaning is to be looked for within nature. The lack of subordination in the sentence makes pleasure a green branch and pain a black branch, as well as allowing that each may have its summer and winter.

—Robert Rehder. *The Poetry of Wallace Stevens*. London: The MacMillan Press Ltd., 1988, pp. 65–69.

GUY ROTELLA ON NATURE'S ROLE IN "SUNDAY MORNING"

[Guy Rotella is Professor of English at Northeastern University and editor of the annual Samuel French Morse Poetry Prize. Rotella earned his Ph.D. at Boston College and is the author of *Reading and Writing Nature: The Poetry of Robert Frost, Wallace Stevens, Marianne Moore, and Elizabeth Bishop*; "Economies of Frost" forthcoming in *The Cambridge Companion to Robert Frost*; and the editor of both *Critical Essays on James Merrill* and *The Collected Poems of Samuel French Morse*. In the Stevens section of a longer book on nature as expressed in the work of several prominent modernists, Rotella points out how, in Stevens' work, nature is often the religion or spirituality that has emerged as a result of the philosophical upheavals of the age of science and the end of the nineteenth century.]

Other poems in *Harmonium* abandon metaphysical pleas or posturings for pure or nearly pure description. These are painterly poems, in which the pleasures of observation and of the resemblances the eye or ear discovers or creates provide sufficient satisfactions in themselves, such poems as "The Load of Sugar Cane" or "Sea Surface Full of Clouds." More often, though, the pressure for metaphysical knowledge asserts itself, either by way of its explicit presence or by the various exertions meant to engineer its absence. Occasionally, as in "Sunday Morning," nature provides a replacement faith for the metaphysics naturalism has erased. The pagan and Christian gods, all the gods, are dead—the poem spends much of its time in killing them off, setting us "unsponsored, free." But the requirements they satisfied persist: we feel "The need of some imperishable bliss," "fulfilment to our dreams / And our desires." The poem offers two substitutes for traditional religion. One is a mode of worship in which the object of worship, the sun, is recognized as a metaphor with no transcendent dimension: "a boisterous devotion to the sun, / Not as a god, but as a god might be." The other also involves natural beauty and change, but now not so much as an object of worship as of appreciation, appreciation for the world as it is, beautiful or pleasant, portentous in its lustres, but ambiguous, always expanding and always going to waste:

> Deer walk upon our mountains, and the quail
> Whistle about us their spontaneous cries;
> Sweet berries ripen in the wilderness;
> And, in the isolation of the sky,
> At evening, casual flocks of pigeons make
> Ambiguous undulations as they sink,
> Downward to darkness, on extended wings.

Those swelling cadences evoke the satisfactions of transcendental feeling while disclaiming any transcendent realm to guarantee them; they consecrate an apt accord between human needs and the sorrows, comforts, and elations nature offers. Such sacraments are rare in *Harmonium*. More typical is the self-deprecating "Anecdote of the Jar," in which nature's ends and ours stay radically disjunct. The jar tames and organizes nature ("It made the slovenly wilderness / Surround that hill"), but it does so at the cost of a lifeless exercise of power:

> It took dominion everywhere.
> The jar was gray and bare.
> It did not give of bird or bush,
> Like nothing else in Tennessee.

Nature, on the other hand, can reproduce; it is alive as no work of art, no human object or product, ever can be. It gives life. But it resists order. Even when colonized and made to straighten up, it sprawls around. Here, no choice is made between the poles of nature and culture; no side is taken. Transcendentalism had promised a Logos or realm beyond to certify the fit between the self, its words, and the world. In *Harmonium*, there is no Logos, no transcendent realm. The fit between the self, its poems, and the world is usually a misfit. In this poem, even the form helps say so: quatrains and consonance give the effect of symmetry, but there is no fixed pattern. Nature is blank and alive. Art is significant and artificial.

Stevens rarely leaves it at that. He keeps watching for the curtains of the world to lift, as in the Dickinson-like "The Curtains in the House of the Metaphysician." Trained to expect transcendent revelations, he sometimes hopes for those; more often he is "bold to see" "Deflations of distance" and to hear, not a heavenly voice, but only the silence dropping. When the final curtain, the veil of "the firmament," lifts away, it "bares" an emptiness "beyond us," "The last largeness." Apocalypse uncovers no new world, just nothingness, an empty sky, a paltriest nude, a blank. In the words of "Cy Est Pourtraicte, Madame Ste Ursule, et Les Unze Mille Vierges," "This is not writ / In any book." Holy Writ, both the Bible and God's other book, the natural world of transcendent revelations, is a lie. In 1907 Stevens wrote about his spring housecleaning: "I went through my things ... and threw away a pile of useless stuff. How hard it is to do it! One of the things was my Bible.... I hate the looks of a Bible.... I'm glad the silly thing is gone."

By the time of *Harmonium*, all of Stevens's bibles were gone or going; religion, transcendental nature, and previous poetry, too, were dead as sources of truth. Only nontranscendental nature and its dissolving round of birth and growth, decay and death, is left. It is a plenum, but one so exhausted of meaning as to sometimes seem a vacuum. *Harmonium* erases other books. Its responses to the blankness it uncovers are diverse. There is disillusioned anguish and anger—a sense of betrayal and loss at being left "unsponsored" in a world the poet had been taught would give him succor. There are delighted discoveries that the burden of the past is dead, ranging from a somewhat self-regarding pleasure in debunking the follies—the pathetic fallacies—of fools and dupes, to the happy recognition that the blank left by the erasure of all authoritative writ can set the poet "free" and grant him both the confidence and the room to write his own "scriptures"—a gift that exacts in exchange for the giving the surrender of every hope of authority and permanence. Finally, there are efforts to restore old satisfactions, either by stripping the world of the layers of falsifying paint that religion, transcendentalism, and prior art applied, or by performing solipsistic feats of unbounded creation, or by seeking substitutes for religion that will be metaphorical but not metaphysical, substitutes that will meet our needs without exceeding our limits. In a sense, *Harmonium* is theatrical, an actor's trunk, "full of strange creatures, new & old." In it the actor rummages around, looking for a costume, a gesture, a voice to suit the role he already has: to discover how to accommodate the loss of absolutes and exercise his freedom in a world completely waste and full of portentous lustres.

—Guy Rotella. *Reading and Writing Nature*. Boston: Northeastern University Press, 1991, pp. 114–116.

B.J. LEGGETT ON THE POEM'S CENTRAL IDEOLOGY IN STANZA VII

[B.J. Leggett is Distinguished Professor of Humanities at the University of Tennessee in Knoxville. Leggett's books include *Wallace Stevens and Poetic Theory: Conceiving the Supreme Fiction* (University of North Carolina Press, 1987); *Early Stevens: The Nietzschean Intertext* (Duke University Press, 1992); Co-editor (with John N. Serio) *Teaching Wallace Stevens: Practical Essays* (University of Tennessee Press, 1994); *Larkin's Blues: Jazz, Popular Music and Poetry* (Louisiana State University Press, 1999). In this excerpt, Leggett traces the influence of Nietzschean philosophy in Stevens work, pointing out how "Sunday Morning" is the best example of a clear "intertextual" reading.]

Of the entire Stevens canon, "Sunday Morning" is the one poem that has best lent itself to intertextual reading, if we take this term in its loosest sense. Walton Litz has characterized it as the only great traditional poem that Stevens wrote, and he says that we learn to read it not by reading Stevens but by reading traditional English poetry (50). A list of other presences that have been detected in the poem includes (most prominently) Wordsworth, Pater, and Keats, and (not surprisingly) Shakespeare, Milton, Tennyson, Coleridge, Arnold, Shelley, Whitman, Emerson, William James, the Pre-Raphaelites, Matisse, and Manet, and (more surprisingly) Hopkins, Dante, Jonson, Marvell, Stravinsky, Thoreau's *Walden*, Poe's "The Raven," and Sterne's *Tristram Shandy*. Nietzsche has been heard as well, most often in the sun-worshipping ring of men in Stanza VII, a passage that has reminded readers of Zarathustra's similar sun imagery. I do not wish to deny any of these presences or to replace them with Nietzsche's presence; one of the marks of the poem is its multiplicity of arguments, voices, moods, and systems of imagery that display at times the strain of their disparity or opposition. Without rejecting, then, the multiplicity in Stevens' early poems on religion and death, I want to read "Sunday Morning" as a Nietzschean text and demonstrate the manner in which its discourse may be seen as "furrowed" (Macherey's term) by the presence not only of Nietzsche, but of other of Stevens' early poems and at least two later ones.

I begin with a coupling of "Peter Quince" and "Sunday Morning," Stevens' first two major poems. I tried to show in chapter 3 the manner in which poems of *Harmonium* may be read as reflecting Apollonian and Dionysian impulses: on the one hand, a concern with the dreamlike and illusory world of appearance, or the manner in which the very landscape embodies what Nietzsche calls a primordial desire for appearance; on the other, a concern with the Dionysian conception of that which exists behind phenomena, the acceptance of a world of becoming. "Peter Quince" is constructed so as to transport its protagonist from the Apollonian state of individuation and ego-consciousness through an intermediate Dionysian orgy of loss of ego to a final state of life affirmation, a version of the oneness of a world perpetually and simultaneously creating and destroying. This description of "Peter Quince" perhaps serves to pull it closer to "Sunday Morning" than it had appeared when it was read as a poem about form in art, but to bring it closer we should note that "Sunday Morning" contains its own version of the Dionysian orgy in Stanza VII and that the poem as a whole constitutes an argument of a kind for our acceptance of the world that is simply assumed at the conclusion of "Peter Quince." "Peter Quince" sets up an opposition between the Apollonian, the individuated existence of the ego, and the Dionysian, which breaks down conventional barriers and offers the experience of the continuity of all existence. The speaker of "Sunday Morning," to bring the lady in the peignoir to this same life-affirming state, must overcome the more severe antagonism of Christianity, and the poem's treatment of Christianity conforms to the operation that Nietzsche calls the transvaluation of all values, the procedure by which he accomplishes what is now termed a deconstruction of a hierarchy of values. (...)

Macherey argues, as we have seen, that the literary text is hollowed by its marginal ideologies, "by the allusive presence of those other books against which it is elaborated" (80). It is "generated from the incompatibility of several meanings" (80), and its inscriptions of these incompatibilities may achieve different forms. One of these is simply the "presence of a relation, or an opposition, between elements of the exposition or levels of the composition" (79). The text may be unaware that its different levels or parts are based on assumptions that cannot coexist, as "Sunday Morning" represses any sense that Stanzas IV, V, and VI depend on rival ideologies that are in conflict. In Stanza IV the speaker answers the woman's anxiety about time by saying that there has been no supernatural paradise "that has endured / As April's green endures." The implication is that the world of being is characterized, paradoxically, by temporality, the world of becoming by a kind of permanence. It also implies that the recognition of this reversal should help us to reconcile ourselves to the earth. Stanzas V and VI, however, depend on the

Nietzschean ideology that death and change are the sources for the perpetual renewal of becoming, that permanence would produce a state of eternal boredom.

This is a part of a larger conflict concerning the nature of death in the poem. Death, which is at one point the "mother of beauty" and the source of "fulfillment to our dreams / And our desires," is at another point the antithesis of the bounty of life: "Why should she give her bounty to the dead?" Images of death in the poem consequently may show up on either side of its being/becoming opposition. In the early stanzas the Christian projection of being is made silent, inaccessible, and generally unattractive by death, which also captures the objects of the temporal world in a "procession of the dead." In the later stanzas the Nietzschean projection of becoming is revitalized and renewed by death, which is the ultimate source of all earthly pleasure. Macherey sees such moments in texts as reflecting the work's attempt to unite different levels of discourse which are incapable of being joined without a seam or a gap, and these moments alert us to the presence of ideologies of which the notion of an unconscious level in the text: "does not *know* itself" (84). If we may speak of an unconscious in "Sunday Morning," it is one that is unaware that it holds contradictory notions, that it both fears death as that which robs life of its meaning and affirms it as that which gives life meaning. Here then is an instance of the poem's Nietzschean text in conflict with other of its intertexts, but, more crucially, we may also find that its Nietzschean text, taken in isolation, is marked by an inherent contradiction that threatens the poem's concluding moment of triumph over Christianity.

What a formalist might see as a meaningful paradox and a poststructuralist like de Man as an instance of the manner in which all texts deconstruct themselves, Macherey would see as an example of the way texts unmask and criticize the ideologies on which they are based. As Raman Selden has written of Macherey's theory, "Ideology is normally lived as if it were totally natural, as if its imaginary and fluid discourse gives a perfect and unified explanation of reality. Once it is worked into a text, all its contradictions and gaps are exposed." The writer "intends to unify all the elements in the text, but the work that goes on in the textual process inevitably produces certain lapses and omissions which correspond to the incoherence of the ideological discourse it uses ..." (41). The speaker of "Sunday Morning" assumes the stance of one who is combating the illusory values of Christian ideology with the "real" values of the world as it is, but the poem's disruptions unmask the speaker's own position as equally an ideology. Or, to put it in terms of Jameson's argument, his "real" is unmasked as equally an "ideal," an unmasking most evident in Stanza VII.

This stanza has been something of a problem from the time of its first publication, when Harriet Monroe apparently found it to be of a different tone from the rest of the poem (*LWS*, 183). Other readers have remarked on the stanza's incongruity, and most recently Sandra Gilbert and Susan Gubar have pointed out that the stanza's "crucial importance" to Stevens is signaled by the fact that "both logically and grammatically, this segment of 'Sunday Morning' does not quite 'fit' into the text's elegant chain of reasoning" (393). I want to argue here that this disruption of the poem's unity sensed by a number of readers can be traced to the fact that the stanza represents the final unmasking of one of its ideologies as an *ideology*, the point at which its Nietzschean intertext most emphatically asserts itself and reveals its own inherent contradictions. The phrase that alerts us to the place of the passage in the poem as a whole is the description of the men's chant of paradise as originating "Out of their blood, returning to the sky." The ring of chanting men is thus the answer to the question raised in Stanza III: "Shall our blood fail? Or shall it come to be / The blood of paradise?" As I suggested in discussing Stanza III, the fact that the question is left unanswered at that point is consistent with the values of becoming that the passage assumes. To suggest that the three-stage evolution from God to man has been achieved, that our blood has become the blood of paradise, is to enter the antithetical mode of thought that is being dismissed here. It is to assume that becoming has a goal or an end, and Nietzsche faces a similar dilemma with his utopian model of the *Übermensch*. The texts of both writers tend to evade this threat to their Dionysian conceptions of an uncertain and chaotic world by treating their ultimate goals for the human world as conditions or attainments always to *be* achieved, as is illustrated when Stevens composes notes *toward* a supreme fiction that, the poem makes clear, can never be exactly realized or even too closely defined. "Notes Toward a Supreme Fiction" is, however, a much more sophisticated treatment of the paradoxical desire to posit ideal values in a world acknowledged as chaotic, and "Sunday Morning" comes close to foundering on this very issue. The poem's actual depiction of a future earthly paradise in Stanza VII is too exactly realized to evade the contradiction that it contains. The poem reveals its status here as a production of ideology rather than as a "perfect and unified explanation of reality." It also reveals that, as an ideological construct, it is fated to create the same kind of ideal realm that it has accused its Christian rival of creating, and this contradiction is inescapably a part of the Nietzschean ideology it incorporates.

To see why this should be so, we must note first that Nietzsche's writings ultimately deny a distinction between a world of ideation and an accessible reality. Christianity is exposed as an interpretation based on a certain set of values rather than an immutable "given." At the same time, however (as Nehamas notes), "our own interpretations of these earlier values embody and carry forth the interests and values through which we are most likely to thrive" (6). All interpretations (and that is all that we have) are derived from sets of values, desires, ideals. The world that succeeds Christianity's world in "Sunday Morning" or in Nietzsche's writings is as much a projection of values as the one it replaces. The opposition is not the ideal versus the real but one version of the ideal versus another. This ideological disruption is not always easily read in Nietzsche's writings on Christianity, but the idealized fictional mode in which the earthly paradise of "Sunday Morning" is depicted exposes it in a classic instance of Macherey's thesis of art's unmasking or self-criticism. In postulating a world of becoming in which nothing is given and everything is an interpretation (in Stevens' terms, a fiction), Nietzsche's and Stevens' texts can displace one interpretation only with another, one fiction with another. Although both attempt to give the impression of affirming *what is* rather than what Christian values have idealized, they do so only to contradict other of their assumptions about the innocence of becoming. This is the contradiction laid bare by Stevens' ring of men in Stanza VII of "Sunday Morning," and it represents a tension between the postulation of an unpredictable world of flux and the achievement of an idealist mental construct that persists in Stevens' writings.

"Sunday Morning" has sometimes been seen as standing aloof from the rest of the Stevens canon, an oddity of sorts never repeated. "No later long poem will ever be so purely archaic and nostalgic at once," Helen Vendler writes (*On Extended Wings*, 55), and in that respect perhaps the poem is unique. To suggest, however, as Price Caldwell does, that Stevens' mythic treatment of nature in "Sunday Morning" contradicts the rest of his career (946) is to ignore the nature of the tension the poem introduces into the canon. Walton Litz states the case for the poem's aloofness categorically: "'Sunday Morning' stands alone among the poems of 1914–16, different from them in both language and mood. It is also an orphan in the larger context of *Harmonium* and in the entire canon of Stevens' poetry" (50). I have tried to uncover a text that reveals the poem's central place in *Harmonium*. I believe it would also be possible to show (although I do not propose to do so here) that "Sunday Morning" is the prototype of an ideological conflict that Stevens' texts return to repeatedly, although it is most often expressed in a form—imagination and reality—that represses or deflects its inherent contradictions.

—B.J. Leggett. *Early Stevens: The Nietzschean Intertext.* Durham: Duke University Press, 1992, pp. 88–89; 119–122.

FRANK LENTRICCHIA ON THE POEM'S CONTRADICTORY VALUES

[Frank Lentricchia received his Ph.D. from Duke in 1966 and is Katherine Everett Gilbert Professor of Literature and Theater Studies at Duke. He has taught at UCLA, UC Irvine, and Rice. His chief interests lie in

American literature, history of poetry, modernism, the aesthetics of reading, and the history and theory of criticism. Recent publications include *Introducing Don DeLillo* (1991), *New Essays on White Noise* (1991), *The Edge of Night* (1994) *Modernist Quartet* (1994), *Johnny Critelli and The Knifeman* (1996), *The Music of the Inferno* (1999), *Lucchesi and The Whale* (2001), *Close Reading: The Reader* (2002), and *Modernist Lyric in the Culture of Capital* (2002). He was editorial chair of *South Atlantic Quarterly* for five years. Lentricchia, in his book on what he contends are the four modernist luminaries, Frost, Eliot, Pound, and Stevens, asserts that the four inherited a similar intellectual tradition that they chose to employ in markedly different ways. In the piece excerpted here, Lentricchia stays mostly within the familial context that shaped "Sunday Morning."]

Garrett Stevens was by most standards an unsuccessful poet, and in the end his failure in business was so disastrous—he went bankrupt—that his son had no choice but to stand on his own. His son's life and career as poet and superb man of business were therefore at once an imitation and stunning transcendence of the father. A brilliant success in two areas (he rose to the vice presidency of a major insurance company), Stevens's bifurcated career was the perfect realization of the contradictory values of his society.

> Complacencies of the peignoir,
> And late coffee and oranges in a sunny chair
> And the green freedom of a cockatoo
> Upon a rug....

In a figure with which he will enter into troubled dialogue to the end of his career, the "she" of the opening lines of "Sunday Morning" is represented as a comfortable woman of class, whose expensive and leisured femaleness Stevens insists upon: By their peignoirs ye shall know them. "Sunday Morning," in its atmospherics and in its ideas, appears to be a conventional poem, very much of its intellectual period: a late-nineteenth-century set piece on behalf of the religion of art that happened to be written in New York City in 1914 and published in 1915, in Harriet Monroe's *Poetry*.

"All New York, as I have seen it, is for sale—and I think the parts I have seen are the parts that make New York what it is." Stevens wrote that in a depressed mood shortly after moving from Cambridge. He found everyday life in New York an exhibition of consumer capitalism, a frustrating spectacle, surreal and narcissistic, with "Everybody ... looking at everybody else— a foolish crowd walking on mirrors." In this setting, all commodities become promises of romance, whispers of fulfillment quite beyond the explicit use of commodities: vehicles of an imagined entrance into an existence (with ourselves as heroes and heroines) definitively more pleasurable than one's own, and available for a price. The world of New York, a "field of tireless and antagonistic interests," is the ultimate marketplace: Stevens called it "fascinating but horribly unreal"— he meant "unfortunately real" because so destructively tempting. Nature is sometimes exempted from this economy of desire, but only because (he notes sardonically) winds and clouds are not "generated in Yorkville" or "manufactured in Harlem."

"Sunday Morning" came at the end of almost fourteen years of mostly unhappy New York life. We cannot locate the elegant interior and woman of "Sunday Morning" there, but we can place Stevens in New York, in shabby elegance, inside a room of his own. The interior decoration in Stevens's apartment bore pictures of what he thought "most real" and (in the heart of the city) out of reach.

> The carpet on the floor of my room is grey set off with pink roses. In the bathroom is a rug with the figure of a peacock woven into it—blue and scarlet, and black, and green, and gold. And on the paper on my wall are designs of fleur-de-lis and forget-me-not. Flowers and birds enough of rags and paper—but no more. In this Eden, made spicy with the smoke of my pipe which hangs heavy in the ceiling, in this Paradise ringing with the bells of streetcars and the bustle of fellow boarders heard through the thin partitions, in this Elysium of Elysiums I now shall lay me down.

The contentment and control Stevens communicates in this journal entry about his protected little apartment veils his feeling of being out of place in a world he can't help but encounter daily on the streets of New York. The world of aesthetic enjoyment, often identified in his journals with experiences of art exhibits and nature—not nature in a vacuum, but nature as a motivated negation of New York: what he walked away from on weekends—this aesthetic world of the weekend is not enough in itself to alleviate the dissatisfaction he felt throughout the workweek. His radical desire was for the aesthetic Monday through Friday, and he got it at night in the privacy of his apartment, in the middle of the city, where decor and furnishings appeared to be freed from the "field of tireless and antagonistic interests." Commodities like rugs and wallpaper, so cherished, are the image of heaven—Stevens called it Eden—and their delights are even more keenly felt thanks to the thinness of partitions that do not block out the sounds of the city.

In Stevens's early letters and journals we are taken into the social kitchen of his poetics, where Ezra Pound's modernist shibboleth "Make it New" becomes "Make it Private": the aesthetic as a lyric process of moving toward the interior, from the real space of the streets of New York to the private space of his room, and then into the psychic space of consciousness (now perilously sealed to the outside); lyric aesthesis, the formation of sensuous impression, as the repression of the seedier side of New York—a process that first transforms the bums in Washington Square into "crows in rainy weather" before taking the final leap into subjective freedom—the atmosphere of an impressionist painting, color abstracted from all objects:

> The other morning as I came home I walked up to Washington Square to take a look at the trees.... I was surprised to find the large number of people who were sleeping on the grass and on the benches. One or two of them with collars turned up & hands in their pockets shuffled off through the sulphurous air like crows in rainy weather. The rest lay about in various states of collapse. There must have been a good many aching bones when the sun rose. The light was thin and bluishly misty; by the time I was in my room it had become more intense & was like a veil of thin gold.

In light of the vocational anxieties Stevens experienced in New York, the journal passage on the rug with the peacock woven into it and the opening lines of "Sunday Morning," placed side by side, unveil a decisive scene for modern American poetry: the author imagining himself as sexual as well as economic transvestite: a liberating impulse that he feels (the impulse, as he wrote in his journal, to be "all dream") but that his male obligations tell him he must not choose. The apocalyptic seventh section of "Sunday Morning" returns us to the world, now phallically renewed:

> Supple and turbulent, a ring of men
> Shall chant in orgy on a summer morn
> Their boisterous devotion to the sun,
> Not as a god, but as a god might be,
> Naked among them, like a savage source.
> Their chant shall be a chant of paradise,
> Out of their blood, returning to the sky;
> And in their chant shall enter, voice by voice,
> The windy lake wherein their lord delights,
> The trees, like serafin, and echoing hills,
> That choir among themselves long afterward.

As a vision of the future this passage is absurd, but Stevens's absurdity is important because it joins mainline American literary visions of male utopias, realms of delicious irresponsibility: certain raft passages in *Huckleberry Finn*, the "Squeeze of the Hand" chapter in *Moby-Dick*, Rip Van Winkle's fantasy in the Catskills of men at play, many things in Whitman and, more recently, the Brooks Range conclusion of Norman Mailer's *Why Are We in Vietnam?* What Stevens imagines for the social future is a place without women; men who work, but whose work cannot be distinguished from homoerotic pleasure; men who work nakedly—and in their nakedness bear no signs, as the peignoired woman bears signs, of social difference. Their nakedness and their arrangement in a ring speak the classless language of fraternity (brothers, but no sisters) and equality. And they chant: collectively they create a fundamental poetry—a devotion to a "lordly" nature that is spun out in the sentimentality of choiring angels, a metaphor wrested from traditional Christianity and transvalued with outrageous deliberation into the music of pagan naturalism. The contradictions of Stevens's early life and poetry—work, poetry, and nature itself, the conventional realm of female authority—are fused in an image of masculine power: Father Nature.

In his Harvard journal Stevens makes this incisive remark, whose immediate target might appear to be popular women poets like Frances Osgood and Lydia Sigourney, but whose true object is genteel culture in America: "Poetry and Manhood: those who say poetry is now the peculiar province of women say so because ideas about poetry are effeminate. Homer, Dante, Shakespeare, Milton, Keats, Browning, much of Tennyson—they are your man-poets. Silly verse is always the work of silly men." Yet the power of those silly men to affect the cultural conscience of their time might be measured precisely there, with Stevens saying, in so many words, that he knew better, and yet while knowing better nevertheless played out his literary youth as if he feared that he just might be one of those silly men who would be denied poetic manhood.

As a student at Harvard, Stevens learned to distrust (in a thickening fin-de-siècle atmosphere) overtly moralizing art. He recoiled from Bryant and the Fireside group because, as he put it, the "New England school of poets were too hard thinkers. For them there was no pathos in the rose except as it went to point a moral or adorn a tale. I like my philosophy smothered in beauty and not the opposite." Philosophy smothered in beauty is nevertheless philosophy, not the opposite of philosophy. Aestheticist theory—"the sensuous for the sake of sensuousness"—Stevens found to be "the most arrant as it is the most inexcusable rubbish." "Art," he argued, "must fit with other things; it must be part of the system of the world. And if it finds a place in that system it will likewise find a ministry and relations that are its proper adjuncts."

Stevens's poetics is therefore not unfriendly to his American predecessor Fireside poets, who would have recoiled from his exotic lushness. He was trying to be a poet who would succeed in donning their mantle of cultural ministry—the cultural power that the Fireside poets had assumed for themselves and wielded throughout the American nineteenth century. It was a mantle of authority that neither the economic nor the aesthetic culture of Stevens's young manhood could have granted. The cultural discourse that Stevens was heir to encouraged him to fantasize the potential social authority of literature as phallic authority, and to desire that poetry should be well endowed with social power inside a social formation that cannot itself permit such endowment. However strained, Stevens's music in "Sunday Morning"—it would be replayed in Picasso, Lawrence, and Eliot—speaks the barbarous desire for natural force, not as escape from culture but for manly literary power within.

—Frank Lentricchia. *Modernist Quartet*. New York: Cambridge University Press, 1994, pp. 131–136.

BEVERLY MAEDER ON RHETORIC AND HIERARCHY IN STEVENS

[Beverly Maeder is a permanent lecturer in American literature at Lausanne University. She received her B.A. in French literature from Brown University and studied French and Comparative Literature at Harvard, then Chinese literature at Harvard, in Taiwan, and at the University of Zurich. These interests came together in a *licence* in French and Comparative Literature, English, and Chinese taken at the University of Lausanne. She completed her doctorate in English at Lausanne, with a doctoral thesis on Wallace Stevens written under the direction of Peter Halter. Maeder examines "Sunday Morning" as a structural inversion rather than re-thinking of heaven and earth. As such, she terms it a confrontation, an "againstness," and considers his reasons for adopting such an approach, especially in light of how often Stevens works to upset assumptions of language and order.]

Even a more ambitious poem like "Sunday Morning" (*CP* 66–70), though it rings with memorable language and sober reflection, belies an againstness that ironically inverts heaven's reward and earth's satisfactions, the top and bottom of the hierarchy, rather than devising a new structuring principle. The poem's several subject positions all confront the divine and spiritual with the earthly and bodily. As Eleanor Cook has observed, "The arguments are obvious and stale. But the implicit homiletics: that is another matter. It is in the area of rhetoric that Stevens does battle, not in the area of dialectic." In particular, Cook detects Stevens' challenge to the language of Milton and the Bible in sections I, V, and VIII. From my perspective here, considering the intensity of the younger Stevens' attempt to integrate metaphors of resemblance into new patterns, sections I, III, V, VI, and VII are particularly interesting. Not by accident, they deal pointedly with questions of theological hierarchy.

Section I illustrates the drift from an appreciation of the here and now to an eschatological-oriented belief. "Complacencies of the peignoir, and late / Coffee and oranges in a sunny chair" first instigate a metonymical and spatial movement. The epicurean woman's whole being is drawn toward another realm, as her "dreaming feet" lead her to the "silent Palestine" of Christ's sacrifice. The final "Dominion of the blood and sepulchre," however, can also be seen as the transformation of the opening coffee and oranges and "sunny chair" induced by the resemblances of metaphor. The woman's sensuous comfort thus finds its analogue in a theological symbol that also has its origins in a bodily life—the wine-and-bread celebration of the Last Supper and the Son's interment.

Picking up the strand of Christ's "blood" and humanity, section III inserts Christ's birth into a double structure. On the one hand, it contains three implied narratives of each of the three divine engenderings. On the other hand, it is a condensed "history" of the evolution of religions: from Jove's motherless "inhuman birth," to the virgin birth of Christ and its "commingling" of our blood, to the possibility of a totally human version.

> Shall our blood fail? Or shall it come to be
> The blood of paradise? And shall the earth
> Seem all of paradise that we shall know?

> The sky will be much friendlier then than now,
> A part of labor and a part of pain,
> And next in glory to enduring love,
> Not this dividing and indifferent blue. (III, 9–15)

On the surface one might say with Adelaide Kirby Morris that given this pattern, the woman "must then admit the possibility of evolution from 'the thought of heaven' to a divinity that 'must live within herself ...'" (*CP* 67) of section II. Yet even Jove is measured by the "human" standard of the "king," the negation of "inhuman" and "no mother," and the pun in "Large-*man*nered" (reutilized in "The Man With the Blue Guitar" IV). The narrative of the evolution of religion depends on personification. In addition, the human "hinds" situate Jove hierarchically. They return to recognize the "commingling" (a seemingly nonhierarchical word) of human and divine that defines Christianity, and thus reinforce the hierarchy of earth and "virginal" blood below, and "star" and "heaven" above. The third stage projects an anthropomorphized paradise into the future, leaving "earth" and "sky" in an ambiguous relation.

The hierarchical bias of religious metaphors seems most confining, however, in the implied narrative of each divinity's engendering. These are clustered around the series of representations of human motherhood that ends by integrating "labor" and "pain" (of both working the land and giving birth) into the speaker's imagined "paradise." The vocabulary of this final vision is redolent with double registers that point to a metaphorical contamination of what Kirby calls the divine "within" by a concern with divine origin in the "sky" and "blue" (Mary's color) of heaven, and the "glory" of paradisal splendor. The semantic organization of the entire section keeps returning to the mutual imbrication of physical and divine, even as the section's statements tend to reject past versions of the birth of divine figures because of their vertical perspective. On the other hand, such verticality imbues the stanza's temporal logic. In the story of the expulsion from the earthly Garden of Eden, paradise is origin and first home, while in the promise of a return to God's presence, paradise is heaven but also end as purpose, not only Montaigne's *bout* but the *but* he disputed. The reverie of the eschatological "Dominion of blood and sacrifice" that closes section I foreshadows the absorption of the mothering metaphor of section III into a vision of end, in a final hope that the "sky will be much friendlier than now." The course of an individual human life, the fertile engendering by and of "our blood," is made subordinate to the eschatological "enduring love" to which it is compared but can no longer attain.

The palliative to "all our dreams / And our desires" is given by the adage "Death is the mother of beauty" in section V. This formulation is so hypnotizing that it imposes the "need for some imperishable bliss" even on maidens' love, the prelude to mothering. Death "makes the willow shiver in the sun," mingling the promise of death with the maidens' love here on earth. When the phrase "Death is the mother of beauty" is taken up again to close section VI, it introduces another conceptual difficulty: death is a "mystical" mother "Within whose burning bosom we devise / Our earthly mothers waiting, sleeplessly." Thus, although the section's image of paradise is an image of earth frozen in a stilled moment, the transcendent, not the earthly, is what preconditions the focus of our desires on the sensuous lives embodied in "Our earthly mothers waiting, sleeplessly." If the personification of death as a mother is a "bosom" / matrix for actual ("earthly") mothers, it creates a vertical tautology equating death as mother of transformed versions of earth with the earth as the engenderer of stilled figurations of (death's) paradise. Each seems the superfluous mimesis of the other. Paradise is earth malformed just as "Malformed, the world was paradise malformed" ("The Pure Good of Theory" III, *CP* 332).

Neither do the dynamic relationships that follow in section VII seem to develop alternative metaphors or an alternative structure. Helen Vendler calls this section Stevens' "poem of the *Götterdämmerung*," a representation of "anachronistic primitivism" in which "prophecies of a new divinity are wistfully and even disbelievingly made."

> Supple and turbulent, a ring of men
> Shall chant in orgy on a summer morn
> Their boisterous devotion to the sun,
> Not as a god, but as a god might be,

Naked among them, like a savage source.
Their chant shall be a chant of paradise,
Out of their blood, returning to the sky; (VII, 1–7)

The archaism of the scene brings us back to our ancestral source as well as to a possible archetypal image of sun worship (already latent in the "sunny chair" of section I). Although Harold Bloom praises this section for the "new order" created out of its "metaleptic reversals of the poem's prior figurations," an order in which followers of the Nietzschean god among man manifest both "origin and purpose," the "return" to the sky can also be read as a repetition of the impeding structure of hierarchicalness found in Stevens' other religious metaphors. The chant denotes idolatry, the submissive worship of a "lord." Its figures are derivative of ancient myth and Judeo-Christian successors of it insofar as they enact stories of "blood," the blood of sacrifice in the chant "of paradise, / Out of their blood, returning to the sky," and the blood of reproductive transmission. Blood seems to be the "natural" but male metonymy of the sensuality and sensuousness of maternal "desire/s" of sections II and VI. The section is an ingrown expression of the larger poem's central figures. But the chief impediment to creating a new structure, it seems to me, is the tautological end implied in this disguised eschatology. Indeed, "returning to the sky" closes the circle of the chant's being "of" paradise—a chant about but also from paradise. For the returning chant originates in paradise as well as in the men's blood; it originates, in sum, in the metaphors men have constructed to form paradise.

Thus not only in minor poems but in this major work in *Harmonium* we find Stevens mining the old theological metaphors even as he tries to debunk them. This metaphor-making depends on "using religious forms to deny religious forms." Stevens' figures rely on anthropomorphism since earth provides the analogues for the divine order. Attempts in "Sunday Morning" to give form to a human-centered vision of sensuous pleasure end up relating them to engendering and dying and to God-centered, transcendent value. The religious metaphors tend to merge the implicit life-narrative into a circle or tautology. Jove and paradise in section II and the return of "men that perish" in the sun's "summer morn" are products of our collective metaphor-making ability or our ability to create ensembles of resemblances. The earth's pleasures are imbricated in rhetorical substitutions that never form any independent pattern but can only deplete the divine by taking an ironic view of the earth as model, as in section VI, or by conceding domination to a metaphor of transcendent power that closes the trope in on itself, as in VII.

—Beverly Maeder. *Wallace Stevens' Experimental Language: The Lion in the Lute*. New York: St. Martin's Press, 1999, pp. 19–23.

"The Idea of Order at Key West"

"The Idea of Order at Key West" gave *Ideas of Order* its title, as it is the poem that most expresses the ideas that would emerge into Stevens' most fully expressed work in later years, the work that would set out his aims and thoughts regarding the role of poetry and its sources. The book appeared thirteen years after *Harmonium*, surprising some of the critics who had written off Stevens' initial publication as a product of an aloof dilettante, or an aesthetic throwback, despite the presence of works such as "Sunday Morning." *Ideas of Order*, once it was published with *The Man With the Blue Guitar*, with its darker character and more abstract notions, was a prelude to the longer poems that would comprise *Transport to Summer*.

"The Idea of Order at Key West" was published in *Alcestis*, a short-lived quarterly that also had a press, which published two of Stevens' books, *Ideas of Order* and *Owl's Clover*. As mentioned in Holly Stevens' edition of *The Letters of Wallace Stevens*, the press also published such poets as William Carlos Williams and Allen Tate. The poem appeared in a group with seven others, and led to a relationship of some importance to Stevens with the editor, J. Ronald Lane Latimer.

The rest of the poem explicates the opening line's enigmatic pronouncement: "She sang beyond the genius of the sea." It also sets the formal meter (iambic), a meter Stevens often employed in more cerebral works. Her act of singing is immediately qualified by the narrator who, with a companion (Ramon Fernandez, we learn in the sixth stanza, a person Stevens has claimed is not real, and is not meant to be anyone of any consequence), notices her. The narrator observes, "The water never formed to mind or voice, / Like a body wholly body, fluttering / Its empty sleeves"—that is, the water never matched the voice, an important distinction for Stevens. She was not creating the *thing*. However, as the ocean mimicked the sound (as Stevens puts it, striking out the possibility that she, the singer, may mimic the ocean), it "caused constantly a cry ... of the veritable ocean." By the end of the stanza, the narrator understands that the woman and the sea are not the same, but they do share a connection.

The next stanza states, "The sea was not a mask. No more was she." Neither covers the other, both are in their revealed states, or perhaps, *articulated* states. However, at the end of the stanza, the narrator points out "it was she and not the sea we heard." Her voice was the difference, the call. The sea they expected, walking along it as they were. The voice is a surprise, out of order, as it were. The surprise in the expected emerges as another force to create order, as the following stanza shows. The narrator says, "For she was the maker of the song she sang. / The ever-hooded, tragic-gestured sea / Was merely a place by which she walked to sing. / Whose spirit is this? we said ..." The answer comes quickly. She had chosen to walk here, and chosen to internalize the scene, the ocean that lay before her, and re-order it in song. In asking whose spirit was there, and in knowing they *had* to ask, the narrator and Ramon recognize that the urge, the song, is important. For Stevens, of course, the woman singing is fulfilling the urge for artistic expression, something Stevens felt all people desired, but that only few could fully complete.

Still, as the narrator points out, the reason for asking after the spirit is that the voice they hear is "more than that, / More than even her voice, and ours, among / The meaningless plungings of water and the wind ..." He makes the distinction that if it was only the sea, that is, only the immediate world, and its sounds, however beautiful, it would only have been "deep air." A loveliness, a "heaving speech," but only sound without order. But, because the voice colored how they experienced the landscape, "It was her voice that made / The sky acutest at its vanishing." Her voice made the moment, gave it whatever poignancy the narrator found, whatever compelled him to render the experience in poetic terms. Furthermore, "She was the single artificer of the world / In which she sang." Thus, as she sang, she created a world that was hers, even though others experienced a part of it. She controlled the creation and thus the world it made, and therefore she made her world. The sea, "whatever self it had," became part of her creation. The narrator and Ramon, then, know the only world she possesses is the one she makes in song.

The idea expressed at the end of the fifth stanza is important to Stevens. Among the many aphorisms collected in *Opus Posthumous*, two (at least) speak to this idea. He wrote, "Poetry is the expression of the experience of poetry," and "It is not every day that the world arranges itself in a poem." The inference in both is that the world, expressed in poetry, is the world as the poet has expressed and ordered it, and is the only world that exists.

The sixth stanza builds on the idea, and the narrator's grappling with it. He asks of Ramon Fernandez, the cipher for anyone he might ask, why the world seemed so arranged after hearing the song, why it seemed that it worked, "Arranging, deepening, enchanting night." Is Stevens having fun with the pathetic fallacy? Is he seriously questioning the change in perspective that art affords? It is also no coincidence that the entire scene unfolds at night, as Stevens' work often reverts to darkness and evening when disillusioned, or when questions of reality and perspective become troublesome. In this case, after the song is heard, the night is lighted, glassy, emblazoned, fiery, and therefore alive. Against it, in the next stanza, Ramon is "pale."

In the next stanza as well come lines that include the poem's most famous phrase: "Oh! Blessed rage for order, pale Ramon, / The maker's rage to order words of the sea ..." That the emotion is rage and not desire, not lust, not more cerebral, indicates Stevens' ideas regarding the artistic and expressive compulsions that characterize a sentient being when confronted with the grandeur of the world. Rage is half madness, and in this case half anger at the inability to fully articulate order. Stevens, in his years between books, in his writing periods and fitful stages of productivity prior to this poem, might have felt it quite plainly.

The singer's rage is to order the "Words of the fragrant portals, dimly-starred, / And of ourselves and of our origins, / In ghostlier demarcations, keener sounds." The scope of such rage is huge: words from the imaginary portals (note the appeal to two senses in the line), as well as of ourselves, of humans, and our origins and the complications that go with it. The order itself is finally characterized as "ghostlier demarcations," the comparison admitting that some demarcations already exist, but that such distinctions are nebulous, minimal, giving little means of separating us from the greater whole. At the same time, only the singer is capable of the "keener sounds," the greater subtleties of distinction. Such subtleties of distinction became, of course, for Stevens the driving force behind the gradual tightening of his stylistic precision as well as the growing abstraction in his poems.

"The Idea of Order at Key West"

WILLIAM W. BEVIS ON THE ESSENTIAL IDENTITIES OF ART AND PERCEPTION

[William W. Bevis retired in 1999 as Professor Emeritus of English from the University of Montana. He received his B.A. from the University of North Carolina at Chapel Hill in 1963, and in 1969 received his Ph.D. in English from the University of California at Berkeley. He is the author of *Mind of Winter: Wallace Stevens, Meditation and Literature*; *Ten Tough Trips: Montana Writers and the West*; *Borneo Log*; and a novel, *Shorty Harris or, the Price of Gold*. In the excerpt, Bevis shows how the closing stanzas of the poem unite self and perception into the unique perspective of art.]

The best illustration of the essential identity of art and perception is in "The Idea of Order at Key West" (1936). In that poem the separation of self and other ("she" and "sea") is bridged twice: first by her, the singer who through her art

> was the single artificer of the world
> In which she sang. And when she sang, the sea,
> Whatever self it had, became the self
> That was her song, for she was the maker.
>
> (*CP* 129)

The artist through an act of imagination unites self and other in a third reality, her song. However, the more surprising move, and the better poetry, occurs in the next stanza when two members of the audience, inspired by the song, are walking back toward town and suddenly see the boats in the harbor in a new way:

> Ramon Fernandez, tell me, if you know,
> Why when the singing ended and we turned

Toward the town, tell why the glassy lights,
The lights in the fishing boats at anchor there,
As the night descended, tilting in the air,
Mastered the night and portioned out the sea,
Fixing emblazoned zones and fiery poles,
Arranging, deepening, enchanting night.

Oh! Blessed rage for order, pale Ramon

(CP 130)

The description of masts, lights, and sea resembles a painting by
Paul Klee (one of Stevens' favorite artists). A work of art by
either Klee or the singer by the sea arranges self and other in a
new construct; likewise a moment of imaginative perception in
the life of two members of the audience arranges self and other
in a new construct. The active perceiver lives a life of art: things
as they are have become things as they are painted. And this
imaginative perception has its oxymoronic metaphors of
geometry and mystery resembling Yeats's "cold and passionate")
that combine in a moment of dazzle: "arranging … enchanting
night." The strong feeling is caught up at the coda: "Oh! Blessed
rage for order." The passionate self creates a new reality through
the secret arrangements, the rage for order present in
imaginative perception, and therefore imaginative perception is
essentially a work of art.

We have noted three aspects of Stevens' concept of self: he
lumps together imagination, thought, feeling, and creative
perception; he finds this compounded self ceaselessly, endlessly
involved in action and reaction within the physical world; and he
believes that the imaginative act of perception is a fact of life as
well as of art. The language that expresses the perceptions of the
active, imaginative self is metaphoric, for metaphor's
superimposition of *A* and *B* ("the sea was glass") to create a third
reality (sea-glass) imitates the imagination's superimposition of
self and other ("the sea … became the self that was her song") to
create reality-as-it-is-lived. The more active and bold the self,
the more dazzling the metaphors and the more imaginative the
final reality:

By metaphor you paint
A thing. Thus, the pineapple was a leather fruit,
A fruit for pewter, thorned and palmed and blue,
To be served by men of ice.
             The senses paint
By metaphor. The juice was fragranter
Than wettest cinnamon. It was cribled pears
Dripping a morning sap.
            The truth must be
That you do not see, you experience, you feel,
That the buxom eye brings merely its element
To the total thing, a shapeless giant forced
Upward.
  Green were the curls upon that head.

(CP 219)

But as much as this imaginative self, a head that has merged with the pineapple it perceives, is admired by Stevens, it is also often questioned. The "motive for metaphor," he sometimes believed, is a desire to escape from a final reality "immenser than / A poet's metaphors" (*CP* 341), a desire to shrink from "The weight of primary noon, / The ABC of being" (*CP* 288). Sometimes he wished to "Trace the gold sun about the whitened sky / Without evasion by a single metaphor" (*CP* 373). As we have observed, Stevens' conception of the self invites a distinction not between this imagining and that, this idea or that, but between more self and less self. The imaginative and meditative models gave him two very different ways of answering what East and West both see as a problem, to say the least: ordinary consciousness, ordinarily does not suffice. In much of Stevens, and in most romantic art, one escapes the ordinary self by developing an extraordinary, more excited self: one escapes to dazzle. But in many Stevens poems, the antidote to ordinary self is not more self, but not-self, immersion of the no-mind in sure, bare perception: one escapes to clarity. Thus meditation, in Stevens, is the complementary opposite of imagination.

—William W. Bevis. *Mind of Winter: Wallace Stevens, Meditation, and Literature.* Pittsburgh: University of Pittsburgh Press, 1988, pp. 147–149.

[In this extract, Rehder discusses the metaphor of the voice as it creates reality within the poem as well as how the voice creates the poet's reality.]

Perhaps it is at the beginnings of our lives, the beginnings of our consciousness, that disembodied voices sustain our reality and pose existence as a problem—a problem that the poet solves by creating a space (the poem) in which voice and body can be united so as to form a real world.

'The Idea of Order at Key West', published in 1934, explores this same metaphor. The poet and a friend (one of the many couples in the poems) walking on the beach at nightfall hear a woman singing beyond the 'mimic motion' and 'constant cry' of the primeval, elemental, ever-changing ocean. Her voice and the voices of her surroundings intermingle and separate in a process that changes the world for the poet:

> It was her voice that made
> The sky acutest at its vanishing.
> She measured to the hour its solitude.
> She was the single artificer of the world
> In which she sang. And when she sang, the sea,
> Whatever self it had, became the self
> That was her song, for she was the maker. Then we,
> As we beheld her striding there alone,
> Knew that there never was a world for her
> Except the one she sang and, singing, made.

Despite their coexistence, the poet concludes that song and sea are essentially independent—

> The water never formed to mind or voice,
> Like a body wholly body,

—and yet he finds that what he heard was not sound alone:

> But it was more than that,
> More even than her voice, and ours, among
> The meaningless plungings of water and the wind,

Theatrical distances, bronze shadows heaped
On high horizons, mountainous atmospheres
Of sky and sea.

The poet's function in this poem is to listen rather than create, a version of the old (inescapable) notion that the muse sings within the poet and that poetry is the notation of that song; and, as in 'Autumn Refrain', the song is both performance and residuum. The poet asks his companion why, when the woman stopped singing and they turned back toward the town, the lights in the fishing-boats at anchor there:

Mastered the night and portioned out the sea,
Fixing emblazoned zones and fiery poles,
Arranging, deepening, enchanting night.

Order—the self—is a lingering music. The need for order is a passion as urgent and strong as anger, a rage that confers a blessing:

Oh! Blessed rage for order, pale Ramon,
The maker's rage to order words of the sea,
Words of the fragrant portals, dimly-starred,
And of ourselves and of our origins,
In ghostlier demarcations, keener sounds.

Perhaps the rage exists because the desire is for ever unsatisfied, because there can be no final order—because the waves are inhuman and never form to mind or voice, although it is not the sea, or sky, but 'words' that are to be ordered. The world even in its disorder is conceived of as language, made and unmade in words. 'The fragrant portals' suggest Keats'

Charmed magic casements, opening on the foam
Of perilous seas, in faery lands forlorn.

and Tennyson's

Yet all experience is an arch wherethrough
Gleams that untravelled world, whose margin fades
For ever and for ever when I move.

The world is a window on the self. The words to be ordered are of the sea, the portals, ourselves and our origins, all of which refer the poem back to our very beginnings, our coming into being and entry into the world. Our knowledge of this remote past is like the shining of a far-away star, as elusive and ineffable as a fragrance, but ineluctably there, the memory of a voice, an underlying, inner music, a residuum. The deep need to come to terms with it is the source of the blessed rage. As in 'Autumn Refrain', the poet discovers the nature of the self in the interrelation between the person and the world. This is Stevens' way of asking and answering the question 'Who am I?' Here he asserts that, the ghostlier the distinctions, the sharper, the more exact and the more poignant: grey words embody the truth of a black and white world, by combining and merging its antithetical elements as well as indicating that much of the power of this world is in its mystery. 'Nuance' means cloudy, *nuageux*.

—Robert Rehder. *The Poetry of Wallace Stevens*. London: The MacMillan Press Ltd., 1988, pp. 142–144.

J.S. LEONARD AND C.E. WHARTON ON STEVENS' DEVELOPING A ROMANTIC THEME

[J. S. Leonard is Professor of English and head of the English department at the Citadel. He earned his Ph.D. in English at Brown University in 1983. Christine E. Wharton is his frequent collaborator. Leonard is the author of *The Fluent Mundo: Wallace Stevens and the Structure of Reality*. Athens: University of Georgia Press, 1988 (with Christine E. Wharton) and the editor of *Making Mark Twain Work in the Classroom*. Durham: Duke University Press, 1999; *Author-ity and Textuality: Current Views of Collaborative Writing*. West Cornwall, CT: Locust Hill Press, 1994 (with Christine E. Wharton, Robert Murray Davis, and Jeanette Harris. In the excerpt, the critics show how Stevens' meditation on a voice ordering the natural world is both an extension and a theoretical treatment of a similar theme in Wordsworth and Coleridge.]

And "The Idea of Order at Key West" (*CP*, 228–30) revises "The Solitary Reaper," converting the wistful emotiveness of Wordsworth's "Will no one tell me what she sings?" to an epistemological meditation on the song's capacity to order the scene:

> Ramon Fernandez, tell me, if you know,
> Why, when the singing ended and we turned
> Toward the town, tell why the glassy lights,
> The lights in the fishing boats at anchor there,
> As the night descended, tilting in the air,
> Mastered the night and portioned out the sea,
> Fixing emblazoned zones and fiery poles,
> Arranging, deepening, enchanting night.

Although the motif is by no means anti-Romantic (the contest between mind and nature being of considerable interest to the Romantics, especially Coleridge), the specific contrast with Wordsworth's less theoretical treatment adds definition to Stevens' theme. "Key West" enlarges Wordsworth's closing emphasis on memory ("The music in my heart I bore, / Long after it was heard no more") into a speculation on the meaning of the experience:

> Oh! Blessed rage for order, pale Ramon,
> The maker's rage to order words of the sea.

Stevens' disparagement of Romanticism itself, coupled with an elevation of feeling and imagination, signals an alteration of the categories. At this point, the vocabulary of Romanticism fails both Stevens and his readers. While he continues in prose comments to try to make headway with reference to the battered opposition of imagination/reality, his poetry has already transposed the duality; as we have seen (in "Notes," "An Ordinary Evening," and elsewhere), "reality" achieves an inclusiveness that mitigates its conflict with imagination. The Romantic dichotomy, as such, is transcended; the poet pursues "the poem of the composition of the whole" (*CP*, 442) on (if not in) his own terms.

—J.S. Leonard and C.E. Wharton. *The Fluent Mundo: Wallace Stevens and the Structure of Reality*. Athens: The University of Georgia Press, 1988, pp. 43–44.

GUY ROTELLA ON NATURE'S TRANSFORMATION

[In this excerpt, Rotella discusses how the poem develops the theme of the poet's ability to transform nature into a version of reality rooted within the poet himself.]

The role of the poet-priest in creating "benign illusions" that can help us to live in a natural world that lacks a transcendent dimension and that deranges every system we set against its chaos is a central subject in *Ideas of Order*. "The Idea of Order at Key West" is its essential poem. It explores the relationship between the human imagination and natural reality in terms of Stevens's desire for a "benign illusion" that would transfigure our lives without ignoring nature's indifference or succumbing to one or another malign "elusion." Stevens had long seen naturalism or solipsism as two possible responses to the departure of the gods from heaven and nature. "The Idea of Order at Key West" continues to consider those views, and it celebrates the imagination's power to transform the meaningless indifference of nature into significant measures. Here, though, that power is not only celebrated but also corrected and, in some of its forms, supplanted.

The implied narrative of "The Idea of Order at Key West" is a conventionally romantic one. The speaker and his rather ghostly companion overhear a woman singing as she walks along the beach. At first the speaker is tempted to discover in her music a romantic unification of singer, sea, and song, a unification familiar from the transcendentalist faith that there is a God or Logos present behind this world to certify that when we sing in harmony with nature we discover and convey a saving knowledge of transforming truth. It is a temptation the speaker resists as he expresses it, and his ambivalence is condensed in the opening line, "She sang beyond the genius of the sea," where the word "beyond" has its traditional transcendentalist connotations *and* denies any possibility of transcendence by insisting on a radical disjunction between the singer's song and the natural world. The speaker's hopes and doubts are also conveyed in his haltingly assertive speech. He shifts from confident declarations (some of them in conflict with others) to qualifications and back again in a kind of blur of precisions: "The water never formed to mind or voice, ... and yet"; "The song and water were not medleyed sound / Even if ..."; "It may be that" nature "stirred" "in all her phrases," "But it was she and not the sea we heard." And so on.

Whatever surviving transcendental hopes the speaker harbors, they are quickly drowned. The opening sections of "The Idea of Order at Key West" define the natural world as an empty force that offers neither comfort nor knowledge. "[E]ver-hooded" and "tragic-gestured," "heaving," "dark," and filled with "meaningless plungings," nature's voice is a wordless cry, a wild and vacuous howl. There is no presence behind or beyond nature; its only truth is chaos. There is, though, an alternative to this naturalistic vision, and the speaker now hears the singer's song as an act of solipsistic creativity so potent that the sea "became the self / That was her song." This moves and even inspires him, and it gives rise to passages of nearly ecstatic celebration. The force of her imagination is impressive; it appears to transmute the "meaningless plungings" of the "veritable ocean" into a meaningful shape, and to do so not only for her, but for her audience as well:

> It was her voice that made
> The sky acutest at its vanishing.
> She measured to the hour its solitude.
> She was the single artificer of the world
> In which she sang. And when she sang, the sea,
> Whatever self it had, became the self
> That was her song, for she was the maker.

As so often in *Ideas of Order*, "piercing" sounds transform nature, as if the world were (or, as Stevens might say, is) measured by the singer's measures. Eventually, the speaker is so elated by the burden of the singer's song that his own speech is transfigured. The halting assertions with which he began the poem become a fluent question rising from interrogation toward avowal:

> Ramon Fernandez, tell me, if you know,
> Why, when the singing ended and we turned
> Toward the town, tell why the glassy lights,
> The lights in the fishing boats at anchor there,
> As the night descended, tilting in the air,
> Mastered the night and portioned out the sea,
> Fixing emblazoned zones and fiery poles,
> Arranging, deepening, enchanting night.

Those passages are a flourish of praise in which a litany of terms— "made," "measured," "artificer," "became," "maker," "Mastered," "portioned out," "Fixing," "Arranging," "enchanting"— commemorates the imagination's ascension over reality. But for all the celebration, the speaker has already begun a "corrective" commentary on the "singer's" solipsism and his response to it. That she is a solipsist is a given: "there never was a world for her / Except the one she sang and, singing, made." Of course, we have only the speaker's and not the singer's word for this. In fact, we never hear the singer's words or music in the poem at all, nor do we hear her comment on them. As several critics have noticed, Stevens made a dramatic shift from female to male figures of imaginative power in these years. The mistrust feminism has taught us to feel in the presence of masculine mufflings and displacements of the female muse might be brought to bear on the poem. However much the singer's ability to transform nature into a humanly satisfying shape moves and even inspires the speaker, he also resists the notion that her song replaces the "veritable ocean" with itself. For her, he tells us, the sea, "Whatever self it had, became the self / That was her song." For a time, this seems to be so for him as well, but a number of matters undermine the idea, until he comes to see her song as added to rather than replacing the world as it is. The speaker's emphasis on the meaningless indifference of the actual sea, and his extended effort to define precisely the relationship of her song to the "veritable ocean," indicates that for him there is a world other than the "one she sang and singing, made," that the sea retained "whatever self it had" no matter how powerful her song.

As the poem moves toward its conclusion, the focus shifts away from the singer's song to its consequences for the speaker. As it does, it becomes clear that the speaker's earlier praise of the singer includes incipient corrections and supplantings of her voice. In the first passage quoted above, for instance, the word "solitude" is a reminder of the cost of a solipsistic response to nature's indifference; similarly, "vanishing" suggests dissolution and loss as well as magical power, and "artificer" hints at fabrication as well as creative skill. From the perspective of the poem's final stanza, those qualifications seem like the speaker's retroactive emendations. In the second passage quoted above this feeling intensifies. Now the song is over and the speaker and his companion move away from it in time and space, turning "toward the town." In one sense, and this is a measure of Stevens's subtlety here, the speaker's praise for the singer's achievement seems magnified; the shaping force of her song appears to persist even after the song is over, so that the lights on the fishing boats "Mastered the night and portioned out the sea." This does suggest an extension of mastery, but in fact the source of mastery is now located somewhere else, probably in the speaker himself. The singer disappears from the poem, and, more dramatically than before, the speaker takes over both her voice and her power to master chaos and resist the night. This is not, I think, a simple or somehow scandalous usurpation. The singer's inspiration of the speaker is never denied, nor is his power any more free of qualifications than hers is: the words "Mastered," "portioned out," "Fixing," and "Arranging" are strongly challenged by the words "fiery," "deepening," and "enchanting," especially the last, with its implication of fraudulent imposition. Nonetheless, just as the speaker's transcendental hopes were drowned, so is "her" claim that solipsistic creativity might provide a satisfactory response to the vacancy of nature. Her song has not replaced the world, and it has not persisted beyond the moment of its uttering. It does, though, inspire another act of ordering, one that celebrates her song *and* replaces it with a new act of ordering that is more inclusive of naturalistic facts.

—Guy Rotella. *Reading and Writing Nature.* Boston: Northeastern University Press, 1991, pp. 119–122.

B.J. Leggett on Nietzschean Perspectivism in the Poem

[Here Leggett discusses the "rage for order"—in the context of several poems as well as in "The Idea of Order at Key West"—as being of a kind with Nietzsche's ideas regarding the imposition of systems and ordering power.]

The artist's "Blessed rage for order," to borrow a well-known phrase from "The Idea of Order at Key West," is sanctioned by the argument that the artist does for nonartists what they would gladly do for themselves were they more gifted. The "mediocre," Ludovici argues, "simply because they cannot transfigure Life in that way, benefit extremely from looking on the world through the Dionysian artist's personality. It is his genius which, by putting ugly reality into an art-form, makes life desirable" (91). What the artist does is not, in this conception, different in kind from what we all do. However, the creative aspect of our ordinary seeing of the world is most often lost on us; the artist by consciously manipulating a medium like language, affirms the very basis of perspectivist theory. In his version of this Nietzschean conception of art Deleuze states, "The activity of life is like a power of falsehood, of duping, dissimulating, dazzling and seducing. But in order to be brought into effect, this power of falsehood must be selected, redoubled or repeated and thus elevated to a higher power" (102–03).

This is the conception of art assumed, for example, in "The Idea of Order at Key West" (*CP*, 128), where the song of the woman on the beach is presumably not different in kind from the speaker's order-making ability to give form to his "veritable" but amorphous world (figured here as the "meaningless" sea) with the important exception that "what she sang was uttered word by word." That is, she represents to the speaker "The maker's rage to order words of the sea" in "ghostlier demarcations, keener sounds." She is the artist whose activity, although it parallels the overcoming of chaos characteristic of all perception, appears more acute, more "spiritual." By raising to a higher power in her song a fundamental activity of all life, she enables the speaker to affirm this creative human quality. He sees that "there never was a world for her / Except the one she sang and, singing, made." She also provides what Ludovici assumes is the highest function of the artist for the audience; she allows the speaker to see the world through the transfiguration that her art provides. The poem ends with the persona speculating on the new appearance of the sea—no longer undifferentiated but "portioned out" and fixed in "emblazoned zones and fiery poles," and it is perhaps significant that he is most engaged by the question why the singing has had its ordering effect. Why should song affect us in this way? His answer, like Ludovici's Nietzschean theory, must make an appeal to a fundamental human instinct for order that art best satisfies with its more imaginative demarcations and sounds. (...)

This does not seem to me a trivializing or merely technical reading, for what it uncovers in poems like "Anecdote of the Jar" and "The Snow Man"—in all the perspectivist texts—is the seam that attempts to piece together the ideologies with which they are composed. These texts' official ideology is the Nietzschean model of a featureless void made intelligible through the arbitrary domination of form, artifice. Unofficially, they must depend on a naive empiricism that posits a less arbitrary world, one in which, for instance, the speaker is capable of making distinctions between what is imposed and what is real. To offer an obvious example, the triad of speaker, jar, and wilderness in "Anecdote of the Jar" parallels almost exactly the triad of speaker, singer, and sea in "The Idea of Order at Key West." In both cases, the poem's persona observes the order-creating effects of artifice. In "The Idea of Order at Key West" the persona says of the singing woman what is implied of the jar—"that there never was a world for her / Except the one she sang and, singing, made." But what world exists for the narrator of this poem who stands on the beach and hears the song?

—B.J. Leggett. *Early Stevens: The Nietzschean Intertext.* Durham: Duke University Press, 1992, pp. 185–186; 205.

CRITICAL ANALYSIS OF
"Notes Toward a Supreme Fiction"

In a letter of rebuke to critic Robert Pack on December 28, 1954, Wallace Stevens says, regarding "Notes Toward a Supreme Fiction:" "We are dealing with poetry, not with philosophy. The last thing in the world that I should want to do would be to formulate a system." Nonetheless, the lengthy and expansive "Notes" is the closest iteration of a "Stevens system" available, and thus has attracted more attention and speculation from critics than possibly any of Wallace Stevens' other poems.

The Cummington Press first published "Notes" as a limited edition chapbook in 1942, and the poem appeared in the collection *Transport to Summer*, which Knopf published in 1947. Stevens stated in a letter that he considered "Notes" to be the most important piece in the book. History has borne out his estimation. The other poems in the book are seldom anthologized.

Stevens considered "Notes" to be thirty poems (some critics have taken to calling the individual poems "cantos"), each one composed of exactly seven unrhymed tercets. The poems are then grouped in three collections of ten, under the aphoristic subtitles, *It Must Be Abstract, It Must Change*, and *It Must Give Pleasure*. Thus, despite Stevens' assertion that "Notes" is not a system, the form of the poem itself is systematic. The meter, iambic again, reinforces the precision bred of such a system.

However, against the overwhelming formal structure of the poem, the "Notes" are just that—discursive and self-referential, circular in their logic and repetitive in their tropes, but with no underlying systematic meaning to accompany the pseudo-allusive and specific references that run through the work.

The poem opens with eight lines addressed to a muse. The lines are not, despite the way the poem appears in print in *Collected Poems*, to Henry Church, a noted philanthropist and friend of Stevens. Church was simply a close friend of Stevens, and the poet felt the dedication of such a work was simply a gesture of admiration, nothing more. As Stevens noted several times, the "supreme fiction" is poetry, and thus the first line, "And for what, except for you, do I feel love?" is addressed to his muse, to the poetry itself, to the confluence of fiction and the urge, the "rage" to make art. The "vivid transparence" poetry brings is "peace." That peace is the supreme fiction, and the claim serves as the poem's introduction.

The first few stanzas make specific reference to "ephebe," or a novice soldier, a young citizen, a reference taken from the ancient Greeks, with which Stevens was familiar from grade school and readings at Harvard. By the end of the poem, Stevens is addressing a soldier, and we can presume that having worked through the notes, the ephebe becomes the soldier. But the first few poems, as Stevens conceived of them, have work to do. The poet tells the ephebe that "Phoebus is dead," and thus the god of sun and poetry is dead (as are all gods in Stevens' poetry). With the gods gone, "there is a project for the sun. The sun / Must bear no name ... but be / In the difficulty of what it is to be." The old ways are out, and here Stevens is providing, knowingly or not, his own echo of Pound's famed modernist dictum, "Make it new."

But to do so requires access to purity, the "first idea." The second poem states that the "celestial ennui of apartments"—that is, the night, and the poet staring at the moon alone—in the night we contemplate the first idea. In outlining the thinking endeavor to lead to the first idea, the poem asks the ephebe to cast off old ways, "As morning throws off stale moonlight and shabby sleep." The pronoun here, "It," which could refer to poetry, the act of thought, the supreme fiction, or the ephebe, achieves exactly the ambiguity on which Stevens depends for the poems to have enough uncertainty that their discursiveness holds the entire structure together, despite the poems being simply and emphatically Notes. The third poem of the section directly describes the effects of poetry: "The poem, through candor, brings back a power again / That gives a candid kind to everything." The other stanzas are quintessential Stevens nonsense about the moon (which he says is what the Arabian is meant to signify). Yet, in the system of Notes and their proximity to one another, the nonsense is of a rhythmic and stylistic kind with the rest of the pieces. It is not surprise, then, when this poem concludes "Life's nonsense pierces us with strange relation."

The next section returns to the topic that, "The first idea was not our own." The stanza invokes Descartes as a symbol for reason, and holds that Eden, that imitation of paradise, produced him. But it was an imitation of a paradise that its occupants could not know; it was "a very varnished green." In a sense, the garden was too perfect. Hence, the need to work toward the idea before it. "From this the poem springs:" the poem says, "that we live in a place / That is not our own and, much more, not ourselves / And hard it is in spite of blazoned days." In the fifth poem of the section, the natural world is resplendent in its autonomy, and the human, the ephebe, orders it: "from your attic window, / Your mansard with a rented piano. You lie // In silence upon your bed. You clutch the corner / Of the pillow in your hand. You writhe and press / A bitter utterance from your writhing, dumb, // Yet voluble violence." Thus, again, the poet is putting the lonely apartment, the solitude, as the locus for poetry, the "rage for order" which "cowes" the creatures whom "time breeds / Against the first idea" and the poet is thus in the figure of a trainer, a ringman, a master of his surroundings.

The next poem reiterates the developing notion of abstraction, the only means of expressing the "first idea." The means of attaining such a perspective are handled in the seventh poem. The poet states, "there are times of inherent excellence," and the individual is privy to "not balances / That we achieve but balances that happen." The lines recall Stevens' aphorism, "It is not every day that the poem arranges itself in a poem." But the poem pushes the idea further. When it happens, the viewer can suddenly see the artifice of reason: "behold / The academies like structures in a mist." The eighth poem follows this notion by asking if man is capable of composing his own "castle-fortress-home" out of logic, not unlike one of the academies poking out of the mist, no doubt. The poet insists, though, that however we labor, we are still but humans: "MacCullough is MacCullough." (Stevens reveals in another letter that using the name McCullough was simply to render humanity more specific.)

The last poem completes the first section with distinct clarity. It states "The major abstraction is the idea of man / And major man is its exponent, abler / In the abstract than in his singular, // More fecund as principal than particle, / Happy fecundity, flor-abundant force, / In being more than an exception, part, // Though an heroic part, of the commonal." The passage is vintage Stevens: word play and humor wrought into a profound statement of theory on poetry, reflexive and repetitive at once. The claim is clear: man is a more powerful idea in the plural than any one man can hope to be. This thought complements the idea of the poetic abstraction versus the experiential particular. Yet, the passage—and the section of ten poems—ends by drawing the ephebe's attention to that which he must render in the abstract, a man in an "old coat" and "sagging pantaloons:" "It is of him, ephebe, to make, to confect / The final elegance, not to console / Nor sanctify, but plainly to propound." In a seeming contradiction, Stevens states that to "plainly propound"—to say it straight—requires an abstraction that will allow one to access the "first idea."

(A note of interest: The man in this final poem of the first section echoes the drunken sailor from "Disillusionment of Ten O'clock," the one who dreams he "Catches tigers / In red weather." He is the only one who sees the world differently, even abstractly. He is here again, completing a theme begun in *Harmonium*.)

Despite Stevens' claim that the Notes are not a system, they do have an arrangement and logic that connects them. The pursuit of understanding is the purpose of the notes, and the supreme fiction is an act of logic, with its roots in the logic and fictions of the legal profession, as Stevens biographer Joan Richardson has pointed out. Thus, the first ten poems complete themselves structurally, even if the arguments resonate and resist final settling.

The next ten sections, under the subheading *It Must Change*, provide vignettes of change in the first three poems. The first is concerned with the arrival of bees among spring flowers and a seraph that views this important change in "erotic perfume." The poet comments upon the scene, which is taken straight from

Romantic poetry: "the distaste we feel for this withered scene //
Is that it has not changed enough. It remains, / It is a repetition."
The next poem concerns the President and his commands for
change, and their futility. Then, in the third poem, the statue of
a General is meant to preserve the grandeur of his achievements.
But it does not change: it is "the nerveless frame / Of a
suspension, a permanence, so rigid / That it made the General a
bit absurd, // Changed his true flesh to an inhuman bronze." The
lawyers and doctors (the learned men of professions) watch it,
and remain unmoved. "Nothing had happened because nothing
has changed." This is not the palpable nothingness of Stevens'
other poems (including "The Snow Man" and "The Course of a
Particular"), but rather is the nothing that is the antithesis of
poetry.

Change begets difference, and the fourth poem discusses the
"origin of change." Here, at the end of the poem, the ephebe is
first referred to as being like the poet: "Follow after, O my
companion, my fellow, my self, // Sister and solace, brother and
delight." Despite Stevens' assertions regarding the structure of
the poem, this telling evocation, so near the precise midpoint of
the work's overall structure, seems to indicate a perception of the
young ephebe and the older poet as required opposites, "cold
copulars" or "two things of opposite natures."

The fifth poem invokes a planter living on a far island who, in
remembering and lamenting the likelihood that he will never
hear a banjo again, is contrasting the paradise surroundings of his
new life with the land he wants to remember. An unaffected man
(as opposed to a "major man") could not have borne the
knowledge and burden of such loss and the memory of such
change. The poem is a sterling example of how Stevens, like
Whitman, could maintain interest and momentum over a broad
poem that contained precise contradictions, even "multitudes."
The nonsense phrasing in the next poem—wherein the "bethou"
is the sound of a catbird—is onomatopoeia, recorded changes
over the span of an afternoon. It fits in the section as reportage
of change, rather than theory on it, rather like poems VI and IX
of the first third.

From poem VII on, the poet again, as in the first third, draws the meditations to a point. The seventh poem returns to the scholars' evening battles, contrasting "the courage of the ignorant man, / Who chants by the book," with "the heat of the scholar, who writes // The book, hot for another accessible bliss: / The fluctuations of certainty, the change / Of degrees of perception in the scholar's dark." In the poem that follows, Nanzia Nunzio, an angel with a nonsense name, confronts Ozymandias, the famous king from the eponymous Shelley poem. When the angel, as spouse, stands naked before him, the king refutes the idea, stating that "a fictive covering" always covers the woman. Under the accumulated weight of previous stanzas, and the connection of fiction to poetry, and poetry to the first idea, we realize the naked woman is sheathed in myth and poetry, changing ideas and perceptions, as is the mythical king.

The penultimate poem describes the changing language of the poet, the orator, and the task of language: "He tries by peculiar speech to speak // The peculiar potency of the general, / To compound the imagination's Latin with / The lingua franca et jocundissima." That language brings together the numerous changing creatures echoed earlier in the poem—colors, seraphs, saints, swans, irises—and notes their "will to change." It describes "volatile world, too constant to be denied, //" (the opposing forces of constancy and volatility echo the necessary oppositions of earlier stanzas) "the eye of a vagabond in metaphor / That catches our own. The casual is not / Enough. The freshness of transformation is // The freshness of a world." The changes are what matters. The section ends on what the ephebe can count on: "Time will write them down."

The language of the poem is arguably at its most lush in the last ten poems, fittingly grouped under *It Must Give Pleasure*. The first piece speaks of the irrational pleasures we derive from unchanging things. But the "difficultest rigor" is the sense of pleasure we get that defies reason, that we must work to "catch." In the end, when trying to render a recollected image or experience, Stevens points out, "There are not things transformed. / Yet we are shaken by them as if they were. / We reason about them with a later reason." In the following poem, later reason is itself applied to the stylized version of autumn evening, presented in a blue woman. In her want, no doubt brought upon by the time of the season, "It was enough for her that she remembered." She may not get right the season itself and its trappings, but she still gains pleasure from the recollection. In the third poem, the evocation of red, of the land in repetitions, is itself a linguistic game of repetition and pleasure. Thus, the first three poems, richly hued and heard, are themselves pleasure recreated. Most importantly, the pleasure is recreated from static, unchanging things. This is marked contrast and contradiction to the previous section.

One might ask whether Stevens intentionally contradicted himself in such proximity, or if his idealization of the "supreme fiction" allowed for such contradiction. He wrote (again, in the aphorisms of *Opus Posthumous*), "Poetry is the expression of the experience of poetry." The experience must change, as he notes in the second section. The importance of recollection is that it accommodates one's changing perspective. Thus, recalling a moment of pleasure derived from an unchanging or constant thing does itself change through the different appreciation made possible in recollection. That poetry is the expression, recalled, of that experience, and Stevens allows for it to become a cycle, change is inherent. As the fourth stanza begins, "We reason of these things with later reason / And we make of what we see"— a clear echo of Wordsworth's famous definition of poetry.

Music, bombast, and lush surroundings again make up the imagery of this poem. The things that give pleasure, that comprise "the marriage-place" thus make them "merry well," as they have had pleasure. The pleasure is made gustatory at the beginning of the fifth poem, and at this point all senses, the routes to pleasure, have been satisfied by the poem. Canon Aspirin is, like MacCullough, only a name to give an idea specificity. In this case, the Canon is a mother whose pleasure comes in her hopes for her children, a selflessness that reacts to the changes in her offspring. That she is present in the following poem makes her one of the few specifics to appear on more than one of the thirty poems. The only others to do so are the ephebe and the "major man," both of whom are evoked in the first section, *It Must Be Abstract*.

Poem VI has the Canon contemplating the "nothingness," (almost always a tangible in Stevens' poems) and as she does so, realizes facts have their limitations. When "the learning of man" pushed past the nothingness of night, man was in the "very material of his mind." In the journey beyond nothingness, he has to choose. Stevens has the man, at the apex of awareness, choose to "include the things / That in each other are included, the whole, / The complicate, the amassing harmony." The abstraction here, poetry, is the inclusive strata, the stuff of the mind underlying nothingness, what he in other poems refers to as "purity."

The next poem follows with his conception of poetry's, and art's, sense of ordering experience and creating the "real" world—the ordered and perceived world. However, in stating that such an endeavor is "As the fox and snake do," Stevens links the urge to instinct, implying that it is natural and not a contrivance. He further points out that to "impose is not / to discover." The poet will not need to impose order because order will reveal itself to him. He is emphatic: "It is possible possible possible. It must / Be possible." Here, her links the underlying order, or truth, beyond "nothingness," with poetry, by labeling it "the fiction of an absolute." Thus, when the first fiction is revealed to the poet, and the poet creates that order, the supreme fiction—where the first fiction meets the rage for order of the poet and renders poetry—is made. The pleasure, here, is implied, as the previous sections have produced connections in pleasure that have led to the moment when Stevens' logical loop is completed.

However, after the revelation, the poet asks, "What am I to believe?" If everything the poet experiences is suspect due to his new knowledge of perspective—and here readers are given the extreme vision of an angel descending—he must ask, "Is it he or is it I that experience this?" If he takes pleasure from this, as he says, and yet he cannot trust it, what is he? "Cinderella fulfilling herself beneath the roof?" That is, blissfully unaware of the better world far from the hearth?

In the penultimate poem, the persona makes himself distinct from the birds, as he "can / Do all that angels can." He is able to enjoy what he orders, what he experiences. The songs are merely work, one of the repetitions, "going round and round." In other words, the static things that happen dependably, and that we can take pleasure in experiencing. He states, "Perhaps, / The man-hero is not the exceptional monster, / But her that of repetition is most master." The routine, the allowance for pleasure from order, the expression of experience—here is Stevens' core.

"Fat girl" is the earth, as Stevens has noted. It is the world, then, that the poet will "find in difference," which is "familiar yet an aberration," that he should "name flatly." The whole world is built of "fiction that results from feeling." The world would not exist were the poets not here to sense and proclaim its order. He writes, "They will get it straight one day at the Sorbonne. / We shall return at twilight from the lecture / Pleased that the irrational is rational, // Until flicked by feeling, in a gildered street, / I call you by name, my fluent mundo. / You will have stopped revolving except in crystal." Thus, when the scholars understand the irrational aspect of the world, it will have long since disappeared, frozen in the stasis of reason.

The epilogue addresses the ephebe as "soldier" now, indicating a process that has completed. He tells the soldier of the war in the mind, its polarities, polarities just revealed in the poem: rational and irrational, ascension and decline, earth and sky, autumn and spring, and so on. The soldier's importance is revealed in the poet's claim that the two are needed. "The soldier is poor without the poet's lines, / His petty syllabi, the sounds that stick, / Inevitably modulating, in the blood." The final lines reveal the roles they play, ending on the notion of "the bread of faithful speech," speech which can be understood in the ideas of order and the first idea, the underlying shadows of the real, only rendered real in lines. In this sense, poetry is a war to discover reality, which is itself the actual war and the actual poetry.

"Notes Toward a Supreme Fiction"

RAJEEV S. PATKE ON THE TITLE'S INFERENCE

[Rajeev S. Patke holds a BA and an MA from the University of Poona, and an MPhil and DPhil from the University of Oxford, where he was a Rhodes Scholar. He is Associate Professor and coordinator of the Postgraduate Studies Programme in the Department of English Language and Literature, National University of Singapore. He also co-edits the department's *Working Papers on Language, Literature, and Theatre.* He has published *The Long Poems of Wallace Stevens: An Interpretative Study* (Cambridge University Press, 1985) and with Robert Lumsden, co-edited *Institutions in Cultures: Theory and Practice* (Rodopi, 1996). In this excerpt, Patke discusses the qualification of the text as made clear by the work's title, and how that clarification informs Stevens' aesthetic statements.]

The title of the poem is characteristic of Stevens in withholding as much as it declares about the form and the purport of form in the 'Notes'. Like Nuances, Ways, Asides, Extracts, Variations, Repetitions, Versions, Illustrations and Prologues (all parts of titles of poems), the plurality of 'Notes' registers no casual synonymity. It points to a doctrine of metaphor as metamorphosis, a parallel to the flux of a world in change. The change of metaphor approaches an ideal of figuration which becomes obsolete no sooner than it is achieved, leaving the desire for the future consummation of a further ideal unassuaged in what is the true health of such desire (cf *NA* 81–2). Thus 'Notes' is less a gesture of modesty than a necessary acknowledgement that the poetic text (like the hieroglyph of the world itself) is never complete, that it is only one among many variants of what can never be put in final terms, but only in 'the fiction of an absolute' (*CP* 404). Poems and poetry are to be seen as process, not product (see *L* 435, 443); 'not the form of an aesthetic but the experience of trying to formulate it' (Tindall 1971: 69).

Such a qualification of the status of the poetic text bears a further nuance. These are 'Notes' neither 'of' nor 'about' but only 'toward', a preposition which is a proposition of arrival, not a statement, even less an assertion. It concedes not a necessary arrival but only the recession of a theoretical possibility, always toward, toward, but never finally there. 'An Ordinary Evening' will describe arrival as 'The brilliancy at the central of the earth' (*CP* 473); in the 'Notes', it is 'a moment in the central of our being' (*CP* 380); and prior to the 'Notes', such a truth is approached in only three poems: 'On the Road Home' (*CP* 203–4), the Heideggerian 'Yellow Afternoon' (*CP* 236–7), and in a trope of reading, 'The House was Quiet and the World was Calm' (*CP* 358–9).

Stevens was wary of describing any approach to a content for the form of what he had chosen to call a 'Supreme Fiction'. In some of his letters he described it in a variety of ways: 'By supreme fiction, of course, I mean poetry' (*L* 407). Later he wrote: 'It is only when you try to systematize the poems in the "Notes" that you conclude that it is not the statement of a philosophical theory ... But these are Notes; the nucleus of the matter is contained in the title. It is implicit in the title that there can be such a thing as a supreme fiction.... I have no idea of the form that a supreme fiction would take' (*L* 430). And then: 'I think I said in my last letter to you that the Supreme Fiction is not poetry, but I also said that I don't know what it is going to be. Let us think about it and not say that our abstraction is this, that or the other' (*L* 438). Clearly, the category could be filled by different orders of mind in varying times and places by a different content. Pater and Arnold had prophesied a future for the aesthetic emotion and for poetry respectively as replacements for the role held traditionally by religion (see Kenner 1975: 72). Santayana had looked forward to the imaginative grandeur of a naturalistic poetry on the Lucretian scale (1970: 21, 35). For the present, Stevens could speak of poetry as his content for the category of supreme fiction with a special emphasis: 'Our own time ... is a time in which the search for the supreme truth has been a search in reality or through reality or even a search for some supremely acceptable fiction' (*NA* 173). Such a notion of fictionality corresponds to 'our habit of transposing into fabrication what is creation' (Bergson in Browning 1965: 48); the man of Valéry's *Eupalinos* too 'fabricates by abstraction' (*OP* 272). Stevens's fiction belongs to this category of necessary fabrications of which Nietzsche had said: 'A belief may be a necessary condition of life and yet be *false*' (in Kaufmann 1974: 356); and which Vaihinger had analysed exhaustively as the order of 'the consciously false', requiring no more than the sort of provisional and pragmatic assent that Stevens lends it (see Vaihinger 1924: lxxiv, IIID).

Such are the nuances implicit in the title, suggestive, but without making explicit or normative the form taken by the poem it leads. In the event, an almost Apollonian determinateness of complex if arbitrary intricacy encloses a supposedly informal set of 'Notes'. The gap between title and poem is linked in oxymoron. Stevens was to note both the outrageously arbitrary limit to length accepted by Valéry in agreeing to write *Eupalinos* (115,800 characters), and the liberating rigour he discovered therein (*OP* 270). The form of the 'Notes' is less fantastic, but considerably more ramified. The units of construction—three parts, ten sections to each part, seven tercets to each section—are antithetical to the traditional linearity of 'The Comedian', the expanding circles of 'Owl's Clover', and the modernist non-linear spiral shape of 'The Blue Guitar'.

—Rajeev S. Patke. *The Long Poems of Wallace Stevens: An Interpretive Study*. Cambridge University Press, 1985, pp. 117–119.

J.S. LEONARD AND C.E. WHARTON ON METAPHOR

[In the excerpt, the critics analyze Stevens' attempt to "decreate" as he professes the need to strip away metaphor.]

In section II of "It Must Be Abstract" in "Notes" (*CP*, 381–82), what imagination decreates is specifically an outdated, overly cognitive compartmentalization—the "naming" of "the truth," a process that Stevens terms "the celestial ennui of apartments." As winter is the preparation for summer, the destruction of such tenements "sends us back to the first idea," the root of metaphors which have become opaque:

> ... and yet so poisonous
>
> Are the ravishments of truth, so fatal to
> The truth itself, the first idea becomes
> The hermit in a poet's metaphors,
>
> Who comes and goes and comes and goes all day.

Cambon tells us in regard to Stevens' poetry: "If metaphor (and, by implication, all of poetry, all of knowledge) is a mere evasion, a 'shrinking from' being, it has no value. If it merely duplicates being, it likewise has no value. The only way out seems to lie in discarding 'metaphor' and confessing our impotence vis-à-vis the purity of being, which is ultimately inexpressible" (*The Inclusive Flame*, 84). But the poetry discloses that at the lowest ebb the "first idea" still inhabits the "poet's metaphors"; metaphor becomes a hermitage for the "central" truth: "The monastic man is an artist" (*CP*, 382). Again and again, what is discovered through the poetry is less a matter of "discarding" metaphor than of examining it, producing the "visibility of thought" described in "An Ordinary Evening." Cassirer says, "The nature and meaning of metaphor is what we must start with if we want to find, on the one hand, the unity of the verbal and the mythical worlds and, on the other, their difference" (*Language and Myth*, 84). Stevens, at the beginning of "Notes," rejecting figurational conventions for the sun, redefines the point toward which verbal and mythical converge: the "muddy centre," the "myth before the myth began" (*CP*, 383)—the metaphorical beneath the conventional, the central fiction of the pre-mythical and the starting point for invention of new fictions, since

> ... not to have is the beginning of desire.
> To have what is not is its ancient cycle.
> It is desire at the end of winter, when

> It observes the effortless weather turning blue
> And sees the myosotis on its bush.
> Being virile, it hears the calendar hymn.
>
> It knows that what it has is what is not
> And throws it away like a thing of another time,
> As morning throws off stale moonlight and shabby sleep.
>
> (*CP*, 382)

This is the expressed decreation of Stevens' poetry: to discard "what is not" (the obsolete/insufficient) in favor of "what is" (the vital image that rejuvenates belief). The clarity of the new day sheds "stale" and "shabby" remnants of night. "A thing of another time" cannot suffice: "the calendar hymn" of the changing seasons of belief figures the imagination's essential decreative/creative activity.

Of this cycle, Alan Perlis finds:

> Language provides an illusion of natural process while the ideas that it embodies attempt, with a futility that Stevens frankly acknowledges, to overcome natural process through transformation.... [I]t is in fact precisely from the tormented center, the "subtle" and ultimately inscrutable center, of the object-in-itself, object-perceived conflict that the poems secrete as vital, yet futile transformations of the object world itself. (*Wallace Stevens*, 16)

Stevens, as Perlis indicates, sees the breach between object and aspect as a source of poetry, proposing in "Notes":

> From this the poem springs: that we live in a place
> That is not our own and, much more, not ourselves.
>
> (*CP*, 383)

But the center of this conflict is not the primal "muddy centre," nor is it the "centre that [we] seek" (*CP*, 373); it is a schism that creates desire. And though the seasonal metamorphoses suffice only temporarily, this does not presuppose futility. The gravitational center, as in "Credences," is a fictive absolute— what draws the eye as we "Trace the gold sun about the whitened sky" and "Look at it in its essential barrenness / ... the barrenness

/ Of the fertile thing that can attain no more"; its issue is "Joy of such permanence, right ignorance / Of change still possible." And the sun—as the locus of integration, center of the solar system, life-source, source of the light which "adds nothing," the inconceivably visible, that which makes visible, the invisible original of lunar light, symbol of summer, mark of high noon, what has been the physical/metaphysical center—is something that exists as it exists for us because it is "believed," as Stevens often says and as the title "Credences of Summer" implies.

> —J.S. Leonard and C.E. Wharton. *The Fluent Mundo: Wallace Stevens and the Structure of Reality*. Athens: The University of Georgia Press, 1988, pp. 33–35.

WILLIAM W. BEVIS ON STEVENS' MEDITATIVE VOICE

[In this piece, Bevis discusses the qualities of Stevens' meditative voice and its importance to his aims in longer poems.]

[U]ndirected openness in the long poems forces us to consider language as medium rather than as statement (after all, "what good were yesterday's devotions?") and to read for transitions ("traverses": where will he go next and how will he get there?). But another aspect of these cloud transformations is less obvious and perhaps more important: there is no irony. The voice of these poems gives itself, sincerely, to any number of contradictory propositions, or to sincerity itself, or to irony, with wholehearted and momentary commitment. Then as each cloud dissolves, the voice lets go. The effect is a remarkable detachment, innocence and openness quite unlike the overriding irony of the voice of "The Waste Land." Eliot is consistently disillusioned, Stevens inconsistently illusioned. Stevens' poems commit themselves over and over again to each moment's perception. Compare Emerson's advice in "Self-Reliance": "Speak what you think now in hard words and tomorrow speak what tomorrow thinks in hard words again, though it contradict everything you say today." If Emerson's hardness seems more fervent than Stevens' wit, it is perhaps because Emerson was ecstatic; Stevens was meditative.

Stevens was writing a poetry of the mind in the act of finding, losing, looking, finding, and losing the sufficient. The process is endless and essentially goal-less. The wandering mind is observed, even indulged: the poem neither directs nor resists vacillations. The individual pieces are complete sentences, meaningful and moving, but the structure is cubist collage. This is the heart of Stevens' style in the long poems. They are as structurally radical as the "field of action" process poems of postmoderns, full of "unbridged transitions" and "brilliant improvisation" (Perloff's terms), but as in jazz, the fragments are expressive. Let us consider one example of this wandering form in a remarkably mercurial section of "Notes toward a Supreme Fiction": "It Must Be Abstract." If we can agree on what happens in the text, then we can argue in subsequent chapters what it means.

Just before this section (VII), Stevens has proposed and dismissed a "giant of the weather," and has come happily back to "mere weather, the mere air." No matter what the giant means, the mood is one of welcome deflation, of going from large to small (probably from transcendental to mundane). The section opens, then, in a sort of exuberant commonsense tone and rhetoric. I will offer the original section entire, and afterward outline its essential structure as I read it. Here, then, is one of the more delightfully slippery sections in Stevens, which can serve as our test case of how and why he changes, how the transitions work and what kind of fragmented poems these are:

VII

It feels good as it is without the giant,
A thinker of the first idea. Perhaps
The truth depends on a walk around a lake,

A composing as the body tires, a stop
To see hepatica, a stop to watch
A definition growing certain and

A wait within that certainty, a rest
In the swags of pine-trees bordering the lake.
Perhaps there are times of inherent excellence,

As when the cock crows on the left and all
Is well, incalculable balances,
At which a kind of Swiss perfection comes

And a familiar music of the machine
Sets up its Schwärmerei, not balances
That we achieve but balances that happen,

As a man and woman meet and love forthwith.
Perhaps there are moments of awakening,
Extreme, fortuitous, personal, in which

We more than awaken, sit on the edge of sleep,
As on an elevation, and behold
The academies like structures in a mist.   (*CP* 386)

Whoever the giant is, he is gone and we first notice the simple diction and an aura of mundane ease: "It feels good.... The truth depends on a walk around a lake." The repetitions and the strings of appositives build a typically Stevens tone of civilized lyricism: "a walk ... a composing ... a stop ... a stop ... certain ... certainty ... a rest." The subject of the stanza is some nearly perfect moment when what will suffice has been found in the easiest way, in the most pleasant place. The three occurrences of "Perhaps" divide the entire section into (1) the scene by the lake, (2) a comment on that scene, and (3) an awakening into some unspecified revelation.

I choose this stanza for a test case because it is not obviously or outrageously disjunct or difficult. It could be read as a fairly consistent exposition of the way intellectual integrations ("composing ... definition growing certain") are satisfying and may lead to more extraordinary insights ("behold"). But reading it that way, I find this mediocre poetry: long, slack, repetitive, with clumsy and unconvincing images of perfection. Instead, I find that within this apparent structure, nuances of tone and modulations of key take over and create the real subject: how the mind changes. Read this way, the section has three themes (A, B, C): A, the theme of rest by the lake; A–B, the bridge in stanza 4, in which the theme of perfect rest is found insufficient through its inherent complacency and theme B is anticipated; B, stanza 5, the complementary opposite of A: perfect rest has become mechanical sterility. Finally, theme C, in stanzas 6 and 7, introduces a totally new experience of awakening (versus rest), without the modulation of a bridge.

My description is clumsy partly because of the double vocabulary of *key* and *theme*. *Key* suffers the limitations of any musical analogy, while *theme* too easily misses the irrational nuances of tone, color, and modulation that move the passage from point to point. We have no good vocabulary for such a slippery, musical language form. A dramatic reading is best, and I will attempt to outline one here. If the reader will imagine possible reactions and alternatives to each phrase of the poem quoted, if one reads each of Stevens' statements as a basis for potential change, one comes, I think, closest to what Stevens was doing:

Stanza		Theme
1	good as it is Perhaps truth a walk around a lake	A casual, spontaneous, easy tone and message: the ordinary will suffice. Sets up the complementary opposite: complacency.
		A
2	body tires stop stop certain	So much stopping approaches entropy. As hepatica and definition grow equally certain, is complacency in bud? The key is not yet changed, but this "inherent excellence" resembles the static simplicity of "Poems of Our Climate." We are nearing an extreme of rest.
3	wait certainty a rest Perhaps inherent excellence	
4	all Is well balances Swiss perfection	Bridge. With "all / Is well" the extreme is reached. Things stop in that direction. The modulation introduces "Swiss," suggesting a new key: this lake scene is becoming too perfect, cute, sterile.
	A–B	

5	music of the machine Schwärmerei balances balances		"Swiss" is taken to its extreme, and the new key is established: "good as it is" has become a mechanical sterility. The schmaltz of this music box is mocked.
		B	
6	meet and love forth- with		We are now so balanced that human passion is also automatic. B is the dominant minor potential of the tonic A.
	Perhaps awakening Extreme personal		A dramatic change of key without modulation, although "love" may have suggested personal awakening. In spite of the parallelism of "Perhaps," the situation has totally reversed: "Awakening" replaces "rest," "extreme" and "personal" replace "balance" and "machine." The expected atmosphere of "familiar" and "forthwith" has changed to the unpredictably fortuitous. This revelation is radically disjunct.
		C	
7	more than awaken behold academies like structures		The theme of revelation has developed rapidly to full expression. A new metaphor is introduced, interrupting the scene by the lake.

"Academies like structures in a mist" is enigmatic: do we behold the academies' truth, or our misty distance from their academics? The vision ends on a strange note, and the curious flavor of that image will provide the transition to the next section, which Stevens begins by playing with Viollet-le-Duc's restoration of Carcassonne:

VIII

Shall we compose a castle-fortress-home,
Even with the help of Viollet-le-Duc?

I would think that at this point Stevens could have taken any number of directions. He chose, however, to react to the forced quality of his image "academies like structures" and to mock its grandiosity. Viollet-le-Duc's own obsessive restoration of the medieval town was much publicized during Stevens' youth, and now "we" set out to "compose" some analogous folly. The awakening revelation has itself quickly dissipated, and the transition to irony seems to depend solely on the characteristics of the image chosen for that revelation: "academies" (as in "Sorbonne") generated ironic humor: "A castle-fortress-home."

The primary argument for such a slippery reading is simple: "Swiss perfection," a music box with quaintly swarming notes, and loving "forthwith" strain our credulity as representations of perfection. Rather, they call into question the idea of perfection itself. And this is exactly the kind of tidy little perfection that comes of a desire for "good as it is," "All is well," and "balances ... balances ... balances." What is fascinating about the section and Stevens' technique is that one's distaste for such inert well-being is *not* anticipated in the text: the idea *self*-destructs. There is no irony in the first three stanzas. We all, I hope, have such moods of lake and flower perfection, and any such mood could be extrapolated to its extreme, then mocked. Stevens allows the thought full play: "The truth depends on a walk around a lake"— see "The Doctor of Geneva" for a thoroughly ironic treatment of "lacustrine man"—and the thought runs its natural course. For instance, I am not claiming that a tone or theme of entropy is developed in stanza 2: "body tires ... stop ... stop ... certain." I am claiming that while the tone is still positive, a totally detached observer could see in the terms of this ideal the seeds of its demise. Entropy is simply one of several alternatives raised by the mood, probably in its essence, certainly as it finds expression. Every thought, every mood, every phrase raises possibilities of which a detached observer may be aware, possibilities that the mind may be about to follow. Such reading is not easy to perform; indeed, it is like a performance in which the pianist, say, is not "getting through" the notes, but "getting into" the piece, recreating each phrase as if it had just been found.

The consciousness behind Stevens' meditations, the ultimate voice of these poems, is that of the most detached observer watching the mind in the act of finding the sufficient insufficient, and vice versa. The speaker is really that part of the mind capable of reporting without involvement or interference the rest of the mind's idle transformations of thought and feeling.

—William W. Bevis. *Mind of Winter: Wallace Stevens, Meditation, and Literature.* Pittsburgh: University of Pittsburgh Press, 1988, pp. 255–260.

DANIEL R. SCHWARZ ON THE INDIVIDUAL MIND IN ACTION

[Daniel R. Schwarz is Professor of English and Stephen H. Weiss Presidential Fellow at Cornell University. He is the author of, most recently, *Imagining the Holocaust* (New York: St. Martin's, 1999), *Reconfiguring Modernism: Explorations in the Relationship Between Modern Art and Modern Literature* (New York: St. Martin's, 1997), *Narrative and Representation in Wallace Stevens* (1993), and *The Case for a Humanistic Poetics* (1991). His book, *Conrad in the Twentieth Century*, is forthcoming from the University of Missouri Press. In this passage, Schwarz begins to set out guidelines for the consideration of a work as loose, diffuse, and seemingly inconsistent as Notes.]

Notes Toward a Supreme Fiction (1942) is perhaps Stevens's greatest poem and the central work for understanding his major themes. With their rapid movements and odd juxtapositions, the individual sections often have the structure of a surrealistic painting. Most of the lines are the iambic pentameter of English speech. Composed of thirty sections, each has seven unrhymed tercets or twenty-one lines. The total of 630 lines gives ten lines for each of Stevens's 63 years. These thirty sections are divided into three equal parts or cantos—subtitled consecutively 'It Must Be Abstract', 'It Must Change', 'It Must Give Pleasure'; each part is composed of ten sections. But 'Must' is really, as we shall see, optative; each part could be subtitled 'It Must be Possible'—or, better, 'If it Were Possible'. The poem also has an opening dedication to Henry Church and an epilogue linking the poet to the soldier.

In his brilliant and idiosyncratic *Ariel and the Police: Michel Foucault, William James, Wallace Stevens*, Frank Lentricchia argues for seeing the political and historical implications of Stevens's work and career. He believes that along with William James and Foucault, Stevens took 'the price of modernity to be the loss of self-determination in the normalizing actions of institutional life' (Lentricchia, 25). According to Lentricchia, 'Stevens inhabits the world of James and Foucault; he is wary of system and surveillance and of the police in all their contemporary and protean guises. But Prospero-like he called upon his Ariel and Ariel rarely failed to respond, sometimes bearing unexpected gifts' (Lentricchia, 26). Reading a few poems with great ingeniousness, he writes an allegory of reading Stevens that stresses Stevens as a closet Marxist who creates in his poems a kind of underground of subversive cultural practices. Aesthetic pleasure, including the writing of poetry, was a way that Stevens freed himself from 'commodity fetishism—the hedonism of bourgeois man bought at the psychic expense of a repression of the economic process which gives rife to commodities' (Lentricchia, 151). Taking Stevens as the poet who has been the paradigmatic example of both New Critical and deconstructive formalism, he restores or resolves the personae of Stevens into a historical and biographical entity, who is a culturally-produced figure expressing the period and tensions in which he wrote. Lentricchia wishes 'to redeem the personal subject of Wallace Stevens for history by thinking about his poems as literary actions' (Lentricchia, 23).

It is where Lentricchia departs from Marxism that I most applaud his effort to stress what he calls 'the issue of personal subject' (Lentricchia, 23) and to place it in its historical context.

But at times it is as if Lentricchia himself were trying to fulfil the first of Stevens's stipulations, 'It must be abstract'. My humanistic bent will take issue with both the abstracting tendency of much of Lentricchia's commentary as well as with his Marxist perspective which argues, 'The new, the original, the spontaneous—that was the source of a vital and pleasurable life: those were the values most denied him in advanced capitalist society' (Lentricchia, 205).

Notes Toward a Supreme Fiction raises essential questions about how we speak about a poem that at first lacks consistent principles of voice, mimesis, and character. Even if we are attentive to the play of language, is there any *alternative* to recuperating the most abstract of poems within our ken of understanding? The answer is, for the most part, 'no'. Should we not then attempt to ground our reading in experiential terms? The poem embodies principles that teach us how to read it. My purpose will be to create a dialogue between recuperating *Notes* in terms of discovering principles of action in the speaker's mind and acknowledging when Stevens is using language as a kind of playful adventure to fulfil his desire for originality and spontaneity. I shall be attentive to the poet-speaker as character and to his quest to discover the supreme fiction. In my reading of *Notes*, I shall stress how Stevens, like Joyce and Lawrence, affirms the personal, not at the expense of the social and political, but as compensation for their inevitable disappointments. What counts in the poem's ontology are individual moments of excellence, perception, understanding, intimacy, tenderness, passion; what counts, too, is the individual mind in action, thinking and imagining at its highest potential. When Stevens conjectures about 'times of inherent excellence', they are moments of individual feeling, such as the perfection of the morning moment when 'the cock crows' and when 'a man and woman meet and love forthwith' and moments of insight when 'We more than awaken' (I.vii). Moments of inherent excellence are a refuge from the world without:

For the sensitive poet, conscious of negations, nothing is more difficult than the affirmations of nobility and yet there is nothing that he requires of himself more persistently, since in them and their kind, alone, are to be found those sanctions that are the reasons for his being and for that occasional ecstasy, or ecstatic freedom of the mind, which is his special privilege. (*NA*, 35)

In 1942 Stevens wanted to create in his work islands from which he could retreat from the pressures of history: 'And for more than ten years, the consciousness of the world has concentrated on events which have made the ordinary movement of life seem to be the movement of people in the intervals of a storm' (*NA*, 20). In a sense, Stevens seeks in a supreme fiction a place of refuge from the raging of war. But in 1942, isn't the very writing of a poem that ignores political issues indicative of Stevens's kinship with Pater and Wilde? It is, I believe, an instance of Stevens's capacity for self-delusion that one can remove oneself from history or remake it as one pleases. History finally speaks, and it indicts Stevens for what he has omitted from his epic poem written during wartime. While Stevens may have thought of himself as sympathetic to the left, his stance and demeanour were conservative and elitist.

Against a background of a world at war—a war that follows on the Depression—Stevens dramatizes the discovery of order in poetry: 'Poetry is a purging of the world's poverty and change and evil and death. It is a present perfecting, a satisfaction in the irremediable poverty of life' (*Adagia, OP*, 193). To some extent, the supreme fiction exists always as possibility, as ideal, in the fecund mind of the poet who might hypothetically be able to create the ultimate fiction, even while knowing that it is impossible: 'The final belief is to believe in a fiction, which you know to be a fiction, there being nothing else. The exquisite truth is to know it is a fiction and that you believe in it willingly' (*Adagia, OP*, 189). Stevens believed that he could produce a fiction that would be as valid for his time as God once had been; lest we laugh, so did Lawrence, Yeats, and Joyce. Had he not written: 'It is not the individual alone that indulges himself in the pathetic fallacy. It is the race. God is the center of the pathetic fallacy' (*L*, no. 479)? Put another way, the supreme fiction is the fiction that we can create supreme fictions.

He proposes his *Notes*—sketchy metaphorical observations, but also musical 'notes'—as an antidote to chaos in the public realm. Stevens vacillates between the poles of aestheticism and ascetism until he discovers that they are more alike than unlike and that their alternative is the actual world, the world of authentic memory and authentic pain. *Notes* is an effort to negotiate between the hedonism of aestheticism and the iconoclasm of asceticism. When *Notes* fails or disappoints, it does so because Stevens does not have enough of an historical sense or a common touch to abandon the protections of either the ascetic or aesthetic masks. Too much has been sublimated and repressed for too long.

In *Notes* Stevens dramatizes the movement of his mind in its process of seeking to define the nature of poetry as the mind vacillates between imagination and reality; between abstraction and specificity; between indeterminacy and completion; between detachment and engagement; between allegory and realism; between irony and desire; between lavishness and starkness; between the need for love and the urge to remain reclused and remote. The mind's movement is the action, and the mind does not move in a linear fashion. *Notes* is characterized by rapid changes in tone and subject, changes that challenge our efforts to locate a persona and to define its argument. Thus Lentricchia has written,

> The effect of later Stevens, especially in the long poems, is of someone discoursing on some tremendous urgency, the thing most needed—poetry, the poem, the supreme fiction: but not a person—without ever being able to make it clear what the thing is, though getting close, without ever experiencing the fulfillment that the thing might bring, though getting tantalizingly dose.... What he is writing is a kind of pre-poetry, a tentative approach to the poem, an enactment of desire not as a state of mind, with all the inert implications of the phrase 'state of mind,' but as movement, and not movement in a straight line, as if he could see the end of the journey, but a meandering sort of motion: desire as improvisational action which gives us a sense of starting, stopping, changing direction, revising the phrase, refining the language, drafting the poem and keeping the process of drafting all there as the final thing because the finished thing can't be had.... Wonderful later Stevens draws his reader into the improvisional song of desire, a writing about itself in the sense that the 'itself' is longing as language eking itself out, each phrase a kind of blind

adventure going nowhere, an infinite and exquisite foreplay.
(Lentricchia, 201–2)

THE MEANING OF THE TITLE

We should examine what Stevens meant by the concept of
Supreme Fiction. Clearly he is playing upon the concept of
Supreme Being and the need we have to have something beyond
ourselves in which to believe. In 'The Noble Rider and the
Sound of Words', a piece he first delivered as a lecture in 1941,
he wrote: '[W]hat makes the poet the potent figure that he is, or
was, or ought to be, is that he creates the world to which we turn
incessantly and without knowing it and that he gives to life the
supreme fictions without which we are unable to conceive of it'
(*NA*, 31).

If *Notes* plays off the traditional notion of God, it implies that
we can replace it as the Supreme Fiction to which we refer as we
seek meaning in our lives. The very idea of *Notes*—notes, not
principles—as well as the concept of fiction, evokes and
undermines the romantic notion that nature expresses God's holy
plan and that a pantheism infuses nature. Notwithstanding some
irony towards the Shelleyan (and Whitmanesque) idea of the
poet as prophet and unacknowledged legislator of the world,
Stevens still finds such a notion attractive in *Notes*. The poet
seeks nobility which he defines as 'a violence from within that
protects us from a violence without. It is the imagination
pressing back against the pressure of reality. It seems, in the last
analysis, to have something to do with our self-preservation; and
that, no doubt, is why the expression of it, the sound of its words,
helps us to live our lives' (*NA*, 36).

Stevens is interested in how and why we believe. Ironically, to
a rereader, the Supreme Fiction is itself the concept that there
might be a supreme fiction in the hurly-burly of the
contemporary world—indeed, in the historical morass—or that
we can propose absolute rules of mustness, as the subheadings—
'It Must be Abstract,' 'It Must Change', 'It Must Give
Pleasure'—suggest, or that such concepts can possibly be pure
and untainted. By having three parts—echoing the Trinity of

Christianity—organized into ten poems each (echoing the Ten Commandments), Stevens calls attention to what he regards as the most flagrant of prior supreme fictions and raises the stakes of his inquiry. It is as if Christianity and the concept of an authoritative, directing Church had to be exorcised as part of creating new fictions. When, in the final canto, III.x, he declares the poem as 'fluent mundo' he has finished his cosmological inquiry, an inquiry which basically argues that the only cosmology that matters derives from a continuing inquiry within the individual imagination about the nature of our experience. What the movement of the poem suggests is the inseparability and even interchangeability of the three categories as well as the impossibility of any category purely and without taint fulfilling the ideal of its title.

It is an irony of 'It Must be Abstract' that the moments of insight are best realized in moments of nominalistic *aperçus*; indeed, 'It Must be Abstract' enacts the impossibility of abstraction and of all shibboleths; once Stevens creates 'abstraction bloodied' (I.vi), as he does in his personae, especially the heroic MacCullough and the Chaplinesque and, perhaps, Whitmanesque old poet in his pantaloons, he *enacts* that abstractions cannot be separated from vignettes, anecdotes, sketches, experiential images of past encounters. The very interruption of the abstract language by multiple synchronic incidents that dramatize the consciousness of the speaker shows how the wooden 'it must be' of the title is less effective than the illustration. A more apt title might be 'It Must be Abstract, but, alas, so Much is Lost by Abstraction'. Indeed, like the Socratic dialogues on which the first canto is modelled—an elder man speaks to a younger disciple about essential truths—it is in the *examples* that the lesson is taught. Or, put another way, the poem inevitably emerges from the rigours of abstraction into moments of life.

Unlike the Trinity, which these three poetic commandments are ironically proposed to replace, we cannot keep them apart, because our experience in this world defies such abstraction. All abstractions are 'bloodied'; if there were no experience, there would be nothing to bloody. If the Supreme Fiction is a poetic alternative to the real world, the reliance on the common language—evoking the emotions and attitudes of ordinary life—shows that the concept of supremacy is neither possible nor desirable. In the final poem of both 'It Must be Abstract' and 'It Must Change', the concept of a Major Man is called into question by the figure of the poet as a kind of hobo, a figure at the opposite end of society from the Major Man, 'The man in the old coat, those sagging pantaloons', who is 'looking for what was, where it used to be' (I.x). Living in the park as if he were a vagrant, 'A bench was his catalepsy, Theatre of Trope'. He has 'The eye of a vagabond in metaphor' (II.x); we think of the figure of the poet in 'The Man on the Dump'. We realize that this is a figure from the Depression, the bard-hobo figure evoked and lyricized by Woody Guthrie, the singer of 'This Land is Your Land'.

If allegory is the trope of belief, metonymy—contiguous substitution of one idea, vignette, or description for another—is the trope of scepticism. *Notes* depends on the lateral analogistic movement of the poet rather than upon his summoning something with value from outside the text which places the object or incident with which it is compared on a vertical dimension descending either from God or from another absolute hierarchy of values. Metonymy is the trope of tentativeness, of inquiry, of proposing comparisons to see if they fit; as further substitutions are made and the ground of the analogy is redefined, metonyms modify and remodify the object of comparison in an endless sequence.

—Daniel R. Schwarz. *Narrative and Representation in the Poetry of Wallace Stevens.* New York: St. Martin's Press, 1993, pp. 146–152.

ANTHONY WHITING ON THE ACT OF CREATING EXPERIENCE

[Anthony Whiting is a noted scholar on Wallace Stevens. In addition to *The Never-Resting Mind: Wallace Stevens' Romantic Irony* (University of Michigan Press, 1996), he has published "Wallace Stevens and Romantic Irony"

(*Wallace Stevens Journal*, 1992), and co-authored *The Web of Friendship: Marianne Moore and Wallace Stevens* with Robin G. Schulze (University of Michigan Press, 1997). In the excerpt, Whiting discusses canto VIII of section II as a passage indicating both the difficulty of creating experiences even when the spirit is engaged in creativity.]

Though Stevens writes of the difficulty of creating, he also, like Schlegel, writes of the moment in which the spirit is endlessly and effortlessly creative. One such moment is described in section II, canto VIII of "Notes toward a Supreme Fiction."

> On her trip around the world, Nanzia Nunzio
> Confronted Ozymandias. She went
> Alone and like a vestal long-prepared.
>
> I am the spouse. She took her necklace off
> And laid it in the sand. As I am, I am
> The spouse. She opened her stone-studded belt.
>
> I am the spouse, divested of bright gold,
> The spouse beyond emerald or amethyst,
> Beyond the burning body that I bear.
>
> I am the woman stripped more nakedly
> Than nakedness, standing before an inflexible
> Order, saying I am the contemplated spouse.
>
> Speak to me that, which spoken, will array me
> In its own only precious ornament.
> Set on me the spirit's diamond coronal.
>
> Clothe me entire in the final filament,
> So that I tremble with such love so known
> And myself am precious for your perfecting.
>
> Then Ozymandias said the spouse, the bride
> Is never naked. A fictive covering
> Weaves always glistening from the heart and mind.
>   (*CP* 395–96)

The canto expresses two opposed activities of the mind. In the first, familiar to us from "The Snow Man," the mind strips away its own concepts. But in this canto Stevens does not leave us contemplating the "nothing that is." The second activity of the mind expressed here is creation. Ozymandias says, "A fictive covering / Weaves always glistening from the heart and mind" (*CP* 396). The two activities are simultaneous and engender a never-ending process. The mind continues to reduce its concepts even as it endlessly creates new ones. ("Always" modifies both "weaves," a word Stevens often uses to designate poetic creation, and "glistening.")

The endless creation of fiction after fiction in the canto can be seen as a rejection of the modernist view of creativity, which would limit the mind to arranging experience but would not allow it to add to experience. But does creative activity in the canto take place at the expense of reality? Are these fictions only Hoon-like creations of the self? The issue is one of art's contents, and it is an issue that Stevens takes up in "Three Academic Pieces."

The images in Ecclesiastes:

> *or ever*
> *the silver cord be loosed, or the golden bowl*
> *be broken, or the pitcher be broken at the*
> *fountain, or the wheel broken at the cistern—*

these images are not the language of reality, they are the symbolic language of metamorphosis, or resemblance, of poetry, but they relate to reality and they intensify our sense of it and they give us the pleasure of "lentor and solemnity" in respect to the most commonplace objects. (*NA* 77–78)

How can images that are "not the language of reality ... intensify our sense of it"? How can art give the mind a sense of the real when art makes no pretense of being mimetic? Stevens, as Carl Woodring writes, refuses to make a final decision regarding the content of art. When he stirs creatively, Stevens "hesitates to seek language that would say whether ... the jar to contain [these stirrings] would hold reason, sensation, feeling, or aesthetic intuition." Do the images in Ecclesiastes intensify our sense of reality because they express sensation? Nature? Stevens does not even speculate in the essay on this question. He simply says that art can intensify our sense of reality and leaves open the basis on which art does this.

In the Ozymandias canto, Stevens suggests that art can offer the mind a sense of engagement with reality even as the mind skeptically questions the basis of that engagement. The ongoing process of reduction and creation leads in the canto to a deep feeling of intimacy with the world. This sense of intimacy is expressed in part through the association of the creative process with sexual consummation and marriage. The opening movement of reduction is depicted as an erotic act of disrobing. "She took her necklace off / And laid it in the sand. /.../ She opened her stone-studded belt. / ... / I am the woman stripped more nakedly / Than nakedness" (CP 395–96). Naked, Nanzia Nunzio asks Ozymandias to consummate their love by clothing or covering her. "Clothe me entire in the final filament, / So that I tremble with such love so known" (CP 396). Ozymandias readily obliges. "A fictive covering / Weaves always glistening from the heart and mind" (CP 396). Through the creative act, Nanzia Nunzio becomes Ozymandias' "spouse," a word used six times in the canto to describe her. (She is also, once, termed a "bride.") The union of Ozymandias and Nanzia Nunzio through the fictions created by Ozymandias symbolizes a deep commitment by the mind to its creations. Stevens suggests that through them the mind "marries" the world it contemplates. But even as the mind expresses its commitment to its fictions, it also acknowledges that these fictions are fictions, "a *fictive* covering / Weaves" (emphasis added). Here, as in Schlegel, the mind expresses a dual attitude toward its creations. Because it is aware that each covering is a fiction, the mind skeptically transcends its creations. Yet the mind's marriage to the world through these fictions suggests that it is at the same time sincerely committed to them. This dual attitude of detachment and commitment is described by Stevens in his well-known aphorism: "The final belief is to believe in a fiction, which you know to be a fiction, there being nothing else. The exquisite truth is to know that it is a fiction and that you believe in it willingly" (*OP* 189). Since the process of creation in the canto is continual, and since the mind marries the world through its creations, the mind's experience of the world in this canto is seen as becoming ever richer and more diverse. With each new fiction, the world is experienced in a different way. As in Schlegel, creative activity here "Increases the aspects of experience" (*CP* 447).

—Anthony Whiting. *The Never Resting Mind: Wallace Steven's Romantic Irony*. Ann Arbor: The University of Michigan Press, 1996, pp. 68–71.

PATRICIA RAE ON STEVENS' "EFFACING HIS MUSE"

[Patricia Rae is currently head of the Department of English Language and Literature at Queens University in Kingston, Ontario, Canada. Her recent publications include *The Practical Muse: Pragmatist Poetics in Hulme, Pound, and Stevens* (Bucknell UP, 1997) and articles in journals including *ELH, Comparative Literature, Twentieth Century Literature, Prose Studies, The Wallace Stevens Journal, Southern Review, Analecta Husserliana, English Language Notes* and *English Studies in Canada*. She is currently completing a book on George Orwell and modernism. In this excerpt, Rae discusses the opening lines of the poem and the meaning of Stevens' treatment of the muse.]

The famous apostrophe that opens "Notes Toward a Supreme Fiction" provides a final example of Stevens's propensity for effacing his muse:

> And for what, except for you, do I feel love?
> Do I press the extremest book of the wisest man
> Close to me, hidden in me day and night?

In the uncertain light of single, certain truth,
Equal in living changingness to the light
In which I meet you, in which we sit at rest,
For a moment in the central of our being,
The vivid transparence that you bring is peace.

(CP 380)

Readers who know "Notes" only by the text of the *Collected Poems* have tended to identify the muse addressed here with the friend to whom Stevens dedicates the poem: Henry Church. This reading depends on the dedication's appearing immediately after the title and before the apostrophe; it is more than slightly compromised by Stevens's wish (respected in *Transport to Summer* but not subsequently) that the dedication appear *before* the title, precisely to "*dissociate* [the apostrophe] from Mr. Church." When we consider the opening of "Notes" in the context of Stevens's other apostrophes to the muse, however, it becomes apparent that the important thing is not the identity of the muse but the fact that it is given no clear identity at all. This being could be anyone or anything that seems other than the subject, so long as it seems at this moment to become one with him; addressed as "*you*" it moves to a place "in the central of *our* being." You is a pronoun without an antecedent, a blank place-holder: anyone. In this sense, the ambiguity that made it *possible* to identify the muse with Church is significant. To put it differently, this muse is a liminal creature, ungendered, neither fiction nor fact, the light in which it appears neither "uncertain" nor "certain." Thus, it reflects the advice the virile young ephebe receives in the opening cantos: like the "first idea" that inspires him (and like Pound's "Image" or Ribot's *conception idéale*), it is neither traced to the subject's "inventing mind as source" nor identified with a "voluminous master folded in his fire" (*CP* 381). The speaker's decision, finally, to embrace the muse is clearly the result of the same kind of world-weary pragmatism that motivates the speaker in "Monocle." From the muted declaration of love in the apostrophe's first line, we know that we are not in the presence of an unbridled passion; the speaker entertains his muse not out of some all-consuming devotion but because that figure is the *only* thing toward which he feels love. He makes it clear, furthermore, that he is not about to use superlatives to describe the wisdom this muse communicates—the implied answer to his second rhetorical question is negative. In the end he embraces the muse simply because he is conscious of the value of her (or his) effect: a perfect, even if only passing, "peace."

—Patricia Rae. *The Practical Muse: Pragmatist Poetics in Hulme, Pound, and Stevens*. Lewisburg: Bucknell University Press, 1997, pp. 139–140.

"The Auroras of Autumn"

Knopf published *The Auroras of Autumn* in 1950, at the time when Stevens' critical reputation was established but making great and rather sudden gains. (The poem itself had appeared two years earlier, in *The Kenyon Review*, one of the finest literary journals in the United States then, and now.) Following three years after *Transport to Summer*, it earned Stevens some of the highest praise of his career. The title poem is the best and most ambitious poem of the collection, and with "An Ordinary Evening in New Haven," comprises the apex of Stevens' poetics and theories after "Notes Toward A Supreme Fiction." Stevens himself noted that the two poems were about his attempts to get ever closer to reality. Whereas earlier poems largely dealt with the work of poetry and perception at "ordering" reality, "The Auroras of Autumn" works to understand reality itself, the *true* reality: that which gives shape to the oft-evoked shadows on the cave wall. Stevens clearly notes the relation of the two poems in letters, but does not speak directly of their sequence, nor of their logical match, to be discussed below.

In the 1954 edition (and in subsequent editions) of *The Collected Poems of Wallace Stevens*, "The Auroras of Autumn" appears directly following "Notes," such that it appears they share the same form. "The Auroras of Autumn" is comprised of ten sections, each of unrhymed tercets, only in this case each section is eight stanzas, not seven. As well, the iambic meter is only occasionally regular, unlike in "Notes."

The title immediately invokes thoughts of age, death, and decay, simply through the mention of autumn. However, the auroras, or lights (most often associated with *Aurora borealis*, or the Northern Lights) bring associations of natural splendor, beauty, and, of course, light shed. The divide between light and death here is a tension running through the poem.

The first tension, however, appears in the poem's first word, a pronoun without a specific antecedent. "This" could be any number of things; it could even refer to the title. However, many critics have read the opening as referring to the "reality" for which Stevens constantly sought, and about which he so often wrote. The reality is elusive, and with the serpent living there, "bodiless," reality is given both a sinister and (oddly) surreal quality. In seeing the aurora, the speaker asks, "is this ... Another image at the end of the cave / Another bodiless for the body's slough?" The reference to Plato's "Allegory of the Cave" asks if, once again, what he the speaker is seeing is indeed reality or just a perceptual version of the actual. Before he finds an answer to the question, he repeats, "This is where the serpent lives." It is clear then, that "this" is the land, the "hills" and "tinted distances." So the serpent lives in both the air and the land that surrounds the poet, that may or may not be the irrefutable "reality."

The next stanza, again using a pronoun, proclaims "This is form gulping after formlessness," echoing Stevens' earlier poems on the attempt to make sense of the world through art, the "rage for order" seen in "The Idea of Order at Key West." The pronoun is thus complicated, with possible antecedents being the world, poetry itself, reality, etc. As the first section develops, however, it is clear that the serpent is in fact the aurora. The aurora would be a band of light, twisting and prismatic, snaking, if you will, across the highest point in the sky. Given the line "These lights may finally attain a pole," and its position following yet another "This," the relation becomes clear. The serpent, the aurora, is a sort of hallucination, a bending of the sun as it reacts with gasses in the atmosphere—"body and air and forms and images" all at once. The metaphor extends into more familiar serpent imagery, the ferns, the rocks, the "black beaded head," the "moving grass, the Indian in his glade," all images of uncertainty, of predation, of threat. (Also, keep in mind that Stevens wrote the poem in 1946 or 1947, when the use of Indians as threat imagery was still, to many, acceptable.) The sentiment of the first stanza is that the poet cannot trust even what he thinks he sees, what he expects is reality: his surroundings. The aurora is the divide between the natural world and the dual realm of imagination and the divine.

Rethinking everything, the next stanza begins, "Farewell to an idea." In the next few stanzas, the ideas of home, mother, and father are bidden farewell. The details of home, however imaginary, are stark in their whiteness, and the mark the stark flowers make is "reminding ... of a white / That was different ... not the white of an aging afternoon." The poet, in trying to remember and, thus, reconstruct time and the home, notes the afternoon as aging. He too is aging. Here, a reality is questioned due to both the passage of time and the change in details and the ability of his memory to reconstruct them. As his attention returns to the aurora, after noting the changes in the home and in the seasons, he notes how "the north is always enlarging the change," how the colors and shape of the aurora (all colors common in Stevens' imagery) are, finally, the color of "solitude." The realization of being alone—reinforced by the question of what is real, and if reality is ultimately individual—coupled with the section's terms of loneliness, puts the speaker at a moment of crisis, seeing change around him and in the sky above.

The next two stanzas dismiss the idea of the mother and father, respectively. In section III, the darkness in the house leaves the speaker and the mother "Only the half they can never possess," the recollected reality of the house. Darkness becomes "a shelter of the mind." Note how their contemplation comes, as it does elsewhere in Stevens' work, in the evening. The poet visits the father at the same time, characterizing him as he who "measures the velocities of change." Some critics have theorized that those velocities of change, so present in the world in which Stevens lived at the time, post-war America and the suburban boom of the middle class, technology, industry, communications and the like, informed the poem. Here Stevens is saying farewell to the father idea within a family, but also to the certainties with which father figures and the ideas of paternity are imbued.

The next stanza brings the parents together in a scene of music and celebration. The musicians "strike the instinctive poem." That is, they play what they feel and observe, not using the poem to dig at perception, nor to find the grist for the "supreme fiction." The end of the section reveals that there *is* no poem, only the people of the family assembled. The music and play, the ordered expression, are really only the life perceived. In this way, the poem makes the statement that we order all perception, thus orchestrating our existence by conducting how it is we see. After all, the poem's the thing; what we see is a poem, order. Do we dig beneath that poem to find the *real* poem?

While the first five sections of "The Auroras of Autumn" seem to transition easily one into another, many critics have remarked at the enigma of section VI. They do so despite the link between the play of section V and the theatre of section VI. Charles Berger (*q.v.*) has theorized that the mysterious section is written with atomic warfare as its subject. Given the time and Stevens' political worries (which were seldom expressed in any clear way in his poetry), the claim is less outrageous than it may at first seem. That the scholar sees the sky this way, or even as the aurora, lights made brighter by the presence of dust in the atmosphere, explains why, at the end of the section, he is afraid. The evocation of the Arctic, however, resonates with the poles in the first section, and the physical facts of the aurora and their dominance in the north, at the pole, striving for the apex.

Interestingly, however, for all the conflagration and violent change described in the imagery of section VI, the persona says, "This is nothing until in a single man contained, / Nothing until this named thing nameless is / And is destroyed." The tangible nothing again has to be contained. Even the crisis of what is viewed, the changes and the huge question of the real, has to be destroyed. It is one of Stevens' bleakest statements of frustration and fear of the inability to attain the real.

Section VII digresses further, asking "Is there an imagination that sits enthroned / As grim as it is benevolent, the just / And the unjust, which in the midst of summer stops // To imagine winter?" The religious overtones here are fairly obvious, with the "imagination" "enthroned" (Stevens has written elsewhere of the imagination being the manifestation of God, and that people evolve their gods, thus making imagination key to the divine) as well as the mention of the creator in the third stanza of this section. The imagination, the "it" of subsequent lines, is also shown "sitting," or as it "leaps through us" (both omnipotent and omnipresent), and, ultimately, shifting. The idea of this imagination is reduced to a thought, "a shivering residue, chilled and foregone / Except for that crown and mystical cabala." The icon of divine power and the notion of a ritualistic doctrine become the limited imagination, or religion. In this section that seems an aside, Stevens is taking on the divine and its crude manifestation, religion, on earth. The aurora, perhaps, is connection.

The poet places the divine in the realm of the imagination, so the final lines are the fate of the divine held in human consciousness: "It must change from destiny to slight caprice." After its "jetted tragedy" (rendering it powerless as tale), and its "stele," (rendering it dead), and its own unmaking in "flippant conversation under the moon," the divine is rendered either dead, gone, or simply reduced. Either way, the effect is to separate the divine and the imagination from the experience of the poem, the aurora. Given Stevens' repeated efforts to put the natural world at the center of his aesthetic concern, and his continual personal musings and inner battles with his religion, the power of stanzas VI and VII reflects the power of this final decision to unite the divine and the natural in a poem.

But section VIII shows a divide, considering the intellectual nuances of the effects of such division. "There may always be a time of innocence," the stanza begins, an abrupt declaration following the arguable corruption of the earlier stanza. "There is never a place," thus innocence is only an idea, not a physical thing. The first place where the idea of innocence prevailed was, of course, Eden, and there it only prevailed for a little while. Stevens goes on to link innocence to philosophy, and to cold. The cold resonates with the winter of section VII, and the notion of the "first idea" from "Notes Toward A Supreme Fiction" is here found in the idea of the "pure principle." Innocence is then a postulate, and its purity makes it roughly analogous to the "first idea." Stevens has thus made a corollary context for the first idea; it requires the pure principal.

The paradoxes continue: "Its nature is its end, / That it should be, and yet not be, a thing // That pinches the pity of the pitiful man, / Like a book at evening beautiful but untrue, / Like a book on rising beautiful and true. // It is like a thing of ether that exists/ Almost as a predicate." Hence, the logic that it predicates the first idea. The intellectual link is also made stylistically. In "Notes," Stevens at one point hammers home, "It is possible possible possible." Here, he says, "But it exists. / It exists, it is visible, it is, it is."

The idea of creation and innocence and the parental images from the beginning come together in a highly self-allusive final stanza, wherein the mother, in the dark, is innocent. She sings and plays an accordion (most instruments in Stevens are seen both as comic and as agents of creation) and creates the time "and place" (despite the earlier assertion that there is no innocent place; even Eden was headed towards the opposite of innocence, at the metaphorical hands of a serpent, no less). Finally, we learn it is the place in which "we breathed." Breath is reality ordered again. Thus, while the persona of the poem has intellectualized the divide between the divine and nature, life and death, the seasons, earth and sky, the order is still understood.

In section IX, the "And" is the connection to the previous stanza, the final one of section VIII. Given the place of innocence, the notion of brothers and landsmen, the detail of a tree, one could find much to defend a reading of the section as having to do with Cain and Abel. They sense winter in the "bare trees and a wind as sharp as salt." They "sense" the "activity of fate." That it is a story of genesis, and the poem deals so explicitly with firsts and creation and innocence, the Cain and Abel story here evoked, in this context, is Stevens being instructive on what happens to innocence with time, and thus what happens with the first idea, with God, and so on? Given how precise Stevens' abstractions could be, and yet how allusive a poet he was (he *is* considered one of the Modernists), it's hard to say for certain whether such elements were part of the writing of section IX. However, the section's tone is one of conclusion, leading readers to the same sorts of thoughts that plague the persona: what next? Where will we be next year, and will the wind be sharp? With the realization of innocence passed, as well as ancestral roots and the ancestral home, the persona looks to the sky, to the aurora, and muses on decline. As the persona notices the stars "putting on their glittering belts" (the aurora) he awaits an end that "may come tomorrow in the simplest word / Almost as part of

innocence, almost, / Almost as the tenderest and truest part."
The "It" is the disaster, perhaps death, perhaps worse. It is
referred to earlier: "Of what disaster is this the imminence"? In
his melancholy, the persona begins to see the aurora as a terrible
omen.

In the final section, the persona's emotions intensify: "An
unhappy people in an unhappy world— / Read, rabbi, the phases
of this indifference. / An unhappy people in an unhappy world—
// Here are too many mirrors for misery. / A happy people in an
unhappy world— / It cannot be." The rabbi, for Stevens, was a
symbol for ancient and friendly wisdom (the rabbi appears in a
number of poems in similar roles). The disconsolate persona
here continues, lamenting the unhappiness, until he comes to the
imperative, asking the rabbi to address the congregation about
the made universe, how it is a "contrivance" of a "never-failing
genius"—a sarcastic lampoon of God—that contains paradoxes
"like a blaze of summer straw, in a winter's nick." The
paradoxical God of section VII is now unfrozen, no longer static,
and instead is made real in the contradictions of nature and the
variety of the world, linking the divine to the earthly and cyclical
as Stevens has done in virtually all of his longer and more
complex work.

"The Auroras of Autumn"

JOSEPH G. KRONICK ON STEVENS' "NEGATING HOME"

[Joseph C. Kronick is Professor of English at Louisiana State University and is the department's Director of Graduate Study. Kronick earned his Ph.D. at the University of California, Los Angeles, in 1981. His book, *Ideology and Narrative in Nineteenth and Twentieth Century American Literature*, is forthcoming. He is also the author of *American Poetics of History: From Emerson to the Moderns*, LSU Press, 1984, and *Derrida and the Future of Literature*, SUNY Press, 1999. In this excerpt, Kronick discusses the poem as one example of Stevens' ability, in later poems, to transcend his family and look at origins without the emotional affectations of earlier poems.]

[I]t is in such late poems as "The Auroras of Autumn" that Stevens' massive strength emerges, breaking through the pessimism of a poem such as "The Comedian as the Letter C" and its nostalgia for "Loquacious columns" (*CP*, p. 41) to an uncompromising awareness of the illusion of the parental home that has nothing to do with either pessimism or optimism:

> Farewell to an idea ... A cabin stands,
> Deserted, on a beach. It is white,
> As by a custom or according to
>
> An ancestral theme or a consequence
> Of an infinite course. The flowers against the wall
> Are white, a little dried, a kind of mark
>
> Reminding, trying to remind, of a white
> That was different, something else, last year
> Or before, not the white of an aging afternoon,
>
> Whether fresher or duller, whether of winter cloud
> Or of winter sky, from horizon to horizon.
> (*CP*, p. 412)

In this, the second canto of the "Auroras," along with the third and fourth cantos, Stevens proceeds to negate the ideas of the home: the mother, and the father. As Joseph Riddel has remarked, "Each beginning again is a turning of an image that repeatedly dismantles the 'ancestral theme' of continuity, of the passage of truth from origin to end or from father to son." The whiteness of the cabin suggests "The dominant blank, the unapproachable" (*CP*, p. 477), a past vacated by the tenants of memory leaving the poet free to imagine the present.

In a rarely discussed late poem, "The Role of the Idea in Poetry," Stevens reexamines the descent of the idea from father to son:

> Ask of the philosopher why he philosophizes,
> Determined thereto, perhaps by his father's ghost,
> Permitting nothing to the evening's edge.
>
> The father does not come to adorn the chant.
> One father proclaims another, the patriarchs
> Of truth.
>
> (*OP*, p. 93)

Meaning inhabits the philosopher's chant, or the poem, as a ghost announcing the presence of other ghosts and other fathers. The idea in poetry is the bloodless abstraction of the patriarchal descent of truth from parent to son, for truth inheres in linear descent. Stevens, however, transforms the diachronic descent of parentage into a synchronic pattern of relation—fathers do not breed sons; they bear the dream of patriarchal order:

> They strike across and are masters of
>
> The chant and discourse there, more than wild weather
> Of clouds that bang lateness on the sea. They become
> A time existing after much time has passed.
>
> (*OP*, p. 93)

Fathers are the masters of language and nature at "the evening's edge," the threshold of the imagination. And their temporal priority is the daily recreation of a myth that places a father at the head of the past and, therefore, at the border of night:

114

Therein, day settles and thickens round a form—
Blue-bold on its pedestal—that seems to say,
"I am the greatness of the new-found night."

(OP, p. 93)

The father is the giant guarding truth and, consequently,
blocking access to the book:

Here, then, is an abstraction given head,
A giant on the horizon, given arms,
A massive body and long legs, stretched out,
A definition with an illustration, not
Too exactly labelled, a large among the smalls
Of it, a close, parental magnitude,
At the centre on the horizon, concentrum, grave
And prodigious person, patron of origins.

(CP, p. 443)

The giant designates the poet as a secondary man condemned to
chant "ancestral themes" of a lost home. But in the final stanza
of "A Primitive Like an Orb," Stevens discloses that the giant is
a figure of language's eccentricity:

That's it. The lover writes, the believer hears,
The poet mumbles and the painter sees,
Each one, his fated eccentricity,
As a part, but part, but tenacious particle,
Of the skeleton of the ether, the total
Of letters, prophecies, perceptions, clods
Of color, the giant of nothingness, each one
And the giant ever changing, living in change.

(CP, p. 443)

"The centre on the horizon" proves to be eccentric, that is,
remote from the center. We know of the poem of the whole only
through the lesser poems, the fragments that make of every
particle an ever-changing giant on an eccentric center. To
remove the giant, who is the father, from his privileged position
is to free language from the regulations of a central control. No
longer "the centre of the horizon," the father now stands, like
Emerson on the "horizon" in "Experience," at the threshold of
the book, but not in it. Like the son, he, too, will be a reader
seeking to recapture words that he can never possess.

—Joseph G. Kronick. "Of Parents, Children, and Rabbis: Wallace Stevens and the Question of the Book." *Critical Essays on Wallace Stevens*, edited by Steven Gould Axelrod and Helen Deese. Boston: G.K. Hall & Co., 1988, pp. 109–111.

RAJEEV S. PATKE ON ELEGY

[In this excerpt, Patke outlines not only how the poem is an elegy, but also how it fits into the sequence of Stevens' longer, more philosophical poems.]

'The Auroras' is Stevens's most perfectly organized long poem. In mood, setting, figurations and form it achieves a greater unity and compactness than any other of his long poems. It is also, in effect, his most sublime effort, sustaining a melancholic grandeur in confronting autumnal presentiments of death and auroral prefigurations of the alien power in nature. The poem is thematically sequent to the 'Esthétique', just as the 'Credences' is a kind of postscript to the 'Notes'. 'Credences' celebrates the fiction of a stasis in summer, in a reality outside the mind and in the earth. It extroverts and externalizes apotheosis from man to nature. The 'Notes' finds fulfilment in the self, the 'Credences' discovers it in a season of 'arrested peace' (*CP* 373). Both poems celebrate momentary victories won by poetry from the 'mals' inherent in the nature of human existence.

The 'Esthétique' and 'The Auroras' are more sombre because they are largely elegiac. Their own acts of retrieval matter less than the losses they count. The 'Esthétique' suffers, in comparison with 'The Auroras', in being disjointed and eclectic in its survey of the failed sublimes of the past. The poem lacks emotional coherence as well as figurative continuity. It regresses to a kind of prodigal's homecoming to a maternal earth. 'The Auroras' disengages and draws back from such sentiment even as it releases and returns the sublime from the realm of the aesthetic to the alien realm of nature. The single image of the *aurora borealis* dominates the inscape of the poet's mind and his poem, precluding the 'sleek ensolacings' (*CP* 327) of the aesthetic.

'The Auroras' is Stevens's nakedest confession of awe and fear in the sight of nature; his final acquiescence to the absence of God from the world of the poem; and his reconciliation with the innocence of the earth, an innocence salvaged past any question of 'evil' by the 'Esthétique'. Its form possesses greater economy than that of the 'Notes'; also, it is less schematic, more easily able to accommodate the large archetypal figurations which enact the meditative drama of the poet's mind on the auroral stage of autumn.

While autumn provides the season and mood, 'the mood in which one sums up and meditates on the actualities of the actual year' (*L* 622), and night the time for meditation, the aurora provides the figure of an unusual reality. The opening of the poem seems to depict the shimmering weavings and unfoldings as a serpent shape. Even this shape is conspicuous through most of the first section only in metonymic association with its 'nest'. The series of demonstratives gesture only at the absence of the serpent from the forms of the earth where it is supposed to live. The oddity about Stevens's serpent is that it is scarcely described at all. It is 'the bodiless', its 'head is air', and its form flashes without the skin. For the rest, we are told that 'eyes open and fix on us in every sky' (these are, presumably, stars); that the earthly forms of the serpent's nest gulp after formlessness; and that the lights may finally attain a pole and find the serpent in another nest. This last item is puzzling. What are 'these lights' if not the auroral lights? And yet, if they are the serpent shape, how can the poet talk of their finding the serpent in another nest? The other possibility is to identify 'these lights' (line 14) with the 'eyes' (line 3). But then, the notion of such lights attaining a pole would make little sense.

If the serpent is the bodiless, invisible inside which has shed the slough of the outside (see Beehler 1978: 629); if it is the intuition of a noumenon dissociating itself from phenomena (see Doggett 1966: 140), then, in either case, the auroral lights become a very uneasy and equivocal image. They would then represent neither the purely bodiless nor the embodied, but a kind of strange inbetweenness. The lights are best understood as the manifestation of an intermediary between the terrestrial and something at the other pole from the terrestrial and all its forms, which is represented by the figure of the absent serpent. The first section can then be seen to practise a duplicity. Given the title, the reader is bound to bring his knowledge of the auroras (whether through books or through personal experience) to the imagery. In positing the figure of a serpent the section induces the reader to identify the auroras with the serpent. But the poem does not actually make any such identification. It leaves the content for its figure of the serpent within the area of suggestion and private association. Hence the role of the serpent figure elsewhere in Stevens becomes relevant in the present context.

A youthful entry of 1906 relishes an image of 'the serpent triumphing, horrible with power, gulping, glistening' (*L* 91, *SP* 165). In 1936, in the African wilderness of 'Owl's Clover', 'Death, only, sits upon the serpent throne' (*OP* 55), and later, we discover 'Concealed in glittering grass, dank reptile skins' (*OP* 65). Such imagery combines the traditional and chiefly Christian associations of the serpent with a kind of primitivist horror to give the figure an aura of potent evil. In 'Like Decorations ...' (1935), the horror of the serpent image gets attached to Ananke, the principle of the necessity of change (*CP* 152). The serpent sloughing off its skin is used in 'Farewell to Florida' (*CP* 117) as an emblem of renewal in change, in bidding goodbye to the tropical luxuriance of *Harmonium*, and as the new note struck by the leading poem of the second edition of *Ideas of Order*. The serpent form of change makes for the north, accepting leafless cold as its true home.

Nearer in time to 'The Auroras', in 1942, 'The Bagatelles, The Madrigals' (*CP* 213) enacts a curiously enigmatic allegory figuring the serpent. The first two stanzas of the poem search for the place where the serpent is hidden, interrogating for its location in snow, crevices and darkness. The remaining four stanzas explain the allegory by translating the serpent presence into the mind of man, baffled by the trash of life in 'winter's meditative light'. The presence is fearsome in its vengeful spite, and it dominates over all types of the life of refusal, waste or denial. It is in the 'Esthétique' that Stevens finally works out the notions of evil and pain in a manner combining traditional associations with those generated within his poetry. Its sixth section (*CP* 318) dramatizes the fable of a ravenous bird continually seeking to ingest a sun which seeks its own perfection. The pair become emblematic of the two aspects of desire: the one never satiated and the other never attaining its goal of perfection, both compelled to ceaseless change.

The serpent figure in 'The Auroras' presents a conflation of this two-faced emblem of desire. As a body casting off skins in repeated renewal, its desire is the change of metaphor, sloughing off past embodiments in its appetite for change and for the 'first idea' (cf Riddel 1980: 30). As master of 'the maze / Of body and air and forms and images' (*CP* 411), the serpent is another version, in Stevens's evolving symbology, for the possession of a first idea which will betoken candour and ease. Even if the idea is fictive and unattainable, a momentary approximation may convert its relentless pursuit into happiness. But 'This is his poison', 'that we should disbelieve / Even that'. Thus the serpent's poison is an externalization of the evil within the mind, what the 'Esthétique' identifies as 'The genius of misfortune' (*CP* 316). Our being is in our minds even as our bodies are in the world; and the false engagements of the mind are the 'evil' of life. Translated into the terms of the different images of 'The Auroras', the serpent's poison (like Satan's pride-born envy and desire for revenge, like his role as the genius of misfortune who tempted mankind to evil by the enticement to knowledge), is dual: the biting urge of the desire for change, which creates dissatisfactions with what is there; the tempting ideal of a 'first idea', which we know we cannot achieve (which we therefore 'disbelieve'), but which still keeps us trapped in the relentless pursuit of desire.

We recollect that the ephebe's project for abstraction to a first idea had taken the sun as a prime instance (at the beginning of the 'Notes'). The sun is also, in a literal way, the origin of the stream of electrons which, in contact with the magnetic field of the earth, leads to the visual display of the auroras (see Mitton 1977: 156). In metaphorical terms, the auroras display a light which is solar in origin, but at one remove. Similarly, the serpent shape glistening in the night air, in being but a metaphor, is at two removes from the first idea of its solar origin. Our disbelief in the possibility of taking the display as a direct manifestation of some such entity as God, and our yet persistent desire to get behind the display of the auroral serpent to some origin or reality or first idea, is the dual poison. The Fall of man is due to the genius of the mind ('fault / Falls out on everything', *CP* 316) trapped in its false engagements with the phenomena of nature. In its last two tercets, the first section questions and withdraws its own engagement in the metaphor of the serpent. The devil of metaphoricity has been raised, but will now be laid to rest. The actual reptilian shape (neither phallic worm nor infernal Satan) is introduced into the poem as a reality independent of the false engagements of the mind and its metaphors. The reptile stands for a life prior to the human (like that of the lion, bear and elephant of the 'Notes': *CP* 384–5).

In such a condition of 'innocence' and freedom from the legacy of Adam and Eve, who made the air a mirror for themselves (*CP* 383), snake, grass and Indian are all true natives of the earth; more sure of the sun, and nearer the aboriginal condition of existence for which the poet in Stevens so often expresses nostalgia.

The entire first section is an allegory for the mind's insatiable impositions on nature: the mind's attempt, as St John, to cure the Back-Ache, to 'face the dumbfoundering abyss / Between us and the object' (*CP* 437). In 1950, in 'St John and the Back-Ache', the serpent figure revives, 'erect and sinuous, / Whose venom and whose wisdom will be one'. The first section of 'The Auroras' humbles its own will to metaphoric change by discovering poison in it. The auroras will not be bodied forth or embodied in human terms. To locate a serpent shape in these northern lights is to ingest their alien order into human symbols. The reptile is freed from its symbolic burden, and given its liberty in the grass. It had been an emblem, a part of an ancestral theme, the Fall of man. All such themes repose in memory, and memory releases its hold over them as the reality of autumn and premonitions of the future make inroads into the possessions cherished by the memory. In this world of weak feelings and blank emotions: 'We stand looking at a remembered habitation. All old dwelling-places are subject to these transmogrifications and the experience of all of us includes a succession of old dwelling-places: abodes of the imagination, ancestral or memories of places that never existed' (*OP* 204).

—Rajeev S. Patke. *The Long Poems of Wallace Stevens: An Interpretive Study*. Cambridge University Press, 1985, pp. 191–194.

CHARLES BERGER ON STYLISTIC PARADOX OF THE POEM

[Charles Berger is Associate Professor of English at the University of Utah. He earned his Ph.D. at Yale University, and is the author of *Forms of Farewell: The Late Poetry of Wallace Stevens* (University of Wisconsin Press, 1985) and is co-editor of *James Merrill: Essays in Criticism* (Cornell). In the excerpt, Berger is foregrounding an apocalyptic reading of the poem; however, before doing so, he describes the paradox of the poem's compact and direct style that, nonetheless, harbors depths of association and reference that will keep at least some information from even the most attuned readers.]

The greatness and the difficulty of "The Auroras of Autumn" arise from the same source: the poem has more overlapping spheres of reference, sustains a wider range of emotional intensity, than any other long poem of Stevens. There is much that will always escape the interpreter of "Auroras," but little sense of evasiveness in the poem. Stevens' rhetoric here is both denser and more direct than in "Esthétique du Mal." The sense of immediate danger is heightened—as presiding image, the auroras are more active than the volcano—and the poet's presence in the scene is augmented. At the same time, this immediacy in no way diminishes the larger threat of apocalyptic violence. For if Vesuvius could waste "in solid fire the utmost earth," then the auroras' power is no less. Clearly, these lights induce a reaction that cannot be explained by recourse to the natural phenomenon alone. Late in the poem, Stevens will declare the auroras "an innocence of the earth," but this does not mean that they are to be regarded only as part of nature. What is their composition, then? This can be posed as a question of sources: from where did Stevens "get" the auroras? "Wherever he found the symbol, whether in literature, or in nature ..." writes Vendler; I would suggest adding history to the list, as perhaps the deepest motivation of all. For, I would argue, what triggered the finding of the auroras by Stevens was not so much a text as an event: the dropping of the atomic bomb, the epitome of all the great explosions prefigured in the volcano's trembling. For just as Stevens could read the volcano as an ancient figure for present calamity, so the auroras merged old and current versions of apocalypse in a dense textual weave. When the books are about to burn, the values they radiate are brightest.

To say that the aerial violence of the war figures crucially in the constellation of meanings represented by the auroras is probably to invite skepticism on the part of even the best readers of Stevens, who, while having long ago abolished for themselves the myth of his emotional detachment, would nonetheless resist any suggestion of topicality where only dark sublimity or generalized angst might reign. And yet, "Auroras" is recognized as a poem relentlessly grounded in presentness: "the confrontation of the present is insisted on over and over ... the eye is not allowed to stray." Even though the poem was written in 1947, the end of the war, not to mention visions of the end produced by the war, can still be considered part of the present. Wherever Stevens might have found the auroras, he would not have had to look far for the source of a phrase such as "gusts of great enkindlings" (canto II), or for the image of a world "on flames." Of course Stevens uses all the rhetorical resources of the apocalyptic tradition (an odd phrase), but these are reimagined, reinvested, through his own sense of being witness to the present moment's threat. As he faces that crisis, Stevens calls into play every aspect of his own poetic arsenal, a career's worth of strategies and stratagems, for the potential destruction of civilization brutally mocks his effort to bring that career to completion.

Apart from the question of multiple referents for the auroras, there is the disturbing issue of their relationship to us—or, rather, the relation we find within us to this emblem of destructive force. Are we to say, along with Yeats: "Whatever flames upon the night, / Man's own resinous heart has fed"? On the other hand, the poem loses much of its force if the auroras are read only as natural signs. The lights glide across all sorts of boundaries between the human and nonhuman, now appearing as something created by us, now appearing alien. The poem's deepest conjectures have to do with the union between human destructiveness and nature's power, as well as the extent to which creativity is implicated in violence. Its deepest pathos arises from Stevens' desire to find a saving innocence in the imagination. Yet there is also a sense in which the poem moves toward a possible transcendence of the vulnerable network of earthbound relationships. For the last canto of "Auroras" speaks of a "never-failing genius" who "lived all lives that he might know," but leaves the object of such knowing unnamed. The importance of this omission is underscored by the fact that every other use of "to know" in the poem refers to knowledge based on familiarity. In canto IX, the brothers "knew each other well"; in canto VII, as Stevens imagines the extinction of our planet, he reflects on how the evidence that "We knew each other well" is sure to be lost. Only a reading of the whole poem can begin to explore what Stevens has left so enigmatic at the end.

—Charles Berger. *Forms of Farewell: The Late Poetry of Wallace Stevens*. Madison: The University of Wisconsin Press, 1985, pp. 34–36.

ANTHONY WHITING ON STEVENS' CHANGING TREATMENT OF FICTIONS

[Here, Whiting discusses the difference in Stevens' attitude toward the distance between perception and reality.]

In contrast to "Notes," "Auroras" asks us to approach the real apart from any namings.

This is where the serpent lives, the bodiless.
His head is air. Beneath his tip at night
Eyes open and fix on us in every sky.

Or is this another wriggling out of the egg,
Another image at the end of the cave,
Another bodiless for the body's slough?
                                        (*CP* 411)

Stevens does not here focus on the destruction of one fiction, the creation of another, and the new sense of reality that results from the invention of a new fiction. He seeks not an "invented world" but the flux of the real apart from any fictions, the serpent "Skin flashing to wished-for disappearances / And the serpent body flashing without the skin" (*CP* 411). Nor is he at all certain that he has found the reality that he seeks. Borrowing an image from Plato, Stevens writes that the body flashing without the skin could be "Another image at the end of the cave" (*CP* 411). Stevens had made the same point in the Ozymandias canto of "Notes." The world is always covered with the mind's fictive weavings. There is always another image at the end of the cave. What is different in "The Auroras of Autumn" is the mind's attitude toward this issue. Instead of accepting and enjoying the "invented world," the mind in "Auroras" expresses only a desire to get outside the cave, to find a reality that is not another image, another "fictive weaving."

   This shift in emphasis from inner to outer raises questions in the later work about fictions and about creative activity that are very different from the questions raised about these two subjects in the earlier poetry. For instance, instead of asking whether the mind can view a construct as the real, Stevens will ask whether a construct, or whether creative activity itself, can direct the gaze of the mind outward, away from that which is created by the mind. He will ask if the outer can be encountered in the absence of any activity of the mind, whether creative or destructive. And he will explore the relation between the larger universe of flux and creative activity when the mind's stance toward its constructs is no longer one of belief. All of these questions point away from the two senses of irony that were described earlier. Attention to the outer runs counter to the subjectivism and isolation of, for example, "Tea at the Palaz of Hoon" or "A Rabbit as King of the Ghosts." The real often seems in the late work too precious, too much desired, for Stevens to withdraw from it. Indeed, so strong is his desire for the real that it persists even at the moment of death, as Stevens movingly attests in the very late poem "As You Leave the Room."

Now, here, the snow I had forgotten becomes

Part of a major reality, part of
An appreciation of reality

And thus an elevation, as if I left
With something I could touch, touch every way.
(*OP* 117–18)

The late focus on the outer can also be seen as a turning away from that aspect of the irony of skeptical engagement in which the mind is seen as being able, through its constructs, to situate itself in the real. What sense of irony, then, does the late poetry express, and is this irony related in any way to romantic irony? Part of the answer to these questions is suggested in Stevens' exploration of the relation between fictions and the outer in his lyric of 1952, "The Poem That Took the Place of a Mountain."

There it was, word for word,
The poem that took the place of a mountain.

He breathed its oxygen,
Even when the book lay turned in the dust of his table.

It reminded him how he had needed
A place to go to in his own direction,

How he had recomposed the pines,
Shifted the rocks and picked his way among clouds,

For the outlook that would be right,
Where he would be complete in an unexplained completion:

The exact rock where his inexactnesses
Would discover, at last, the view toward which they had edged,

Where he could lie and, gazing down at the sea,
Recognize his unique and solitary home.

(CP 512)

—Anthony Whiting. *The Never Resting Mind: Wallace Stevens' Romantic Irony.* Ann Arbor: The University of Michigan Press, 1996, pp. 163–165.

GEORGE S. LENSING ON THE POEM'S DISCURSIVE STRUCTURE

[George S. Lensing is Professor of English at The University of North Carolina at Chapel Hill. He is the author of *Wallace Stevens and the Seasons,* Louisiana State University Press, 2001, and *Wallace Stevens: A Poet's Growth*, LSU Press, 1991. In the excerpt, Lensing outlines the points of breakdown and digression in the poem, and discusses their importance to understanding the complications of Stevens' mission to understand reality.]

Of all of Stevens' long poems, "The Auroras of Autumn" (*CP* 411–21) is among his most discursive and private. (I do not agree with Bloom, who speaks of its 'compression' and 'economy.')[71] It was begun apparently with the original encouragement of R. P. Blackmur and appeared in the *Kenyon Review* early in 1948. The poem shares the technique of his other long works: the definition of a particular state of mind by the use of both abstract discourse and poetic parable. There is the use of demonstrative fixities ("This is where ..." [I]; "There may be always a time of innocence. / There is never a place" [VIII]); uncertain antecedents ("They are together, here, and it is warm" [III]: "It is a theatre floating through the clouds" [VI]); occasional allusions that appear incorrigibly private, such as the reference to Chatillon in canto V; allegorical figures, characters, and episodes that metamorphose and merge—many of them taking shape in the poet's mind as he sees them in the motions of the aurora borealis (serpent, cabin, mother, father, theater, festival, unhappy people, happy people). As Joseph Riddel says, "The rhetoric is directed inward rather than outward. The reader overhears rather than hears."[72]

For all its disparity, the poem consistently discloses a process of atrophy and breakdown. In canto I, for example, the serpent, "bodiless," is presented as "gulping after formlessness" and "wished-for disappearances." As Vendler summarizes, "Stevens here bids farewell to the idea which engendered *Credences of Summer*—the idea that one could give credence to summer, that the mind could lay by its trouble, that honey could be hived and a festival held."[73] (Though honey and festival do appear in "The Auroras of Autumn," the images are redefined.) The whiteness of the deserted cabin, flowers, and sand in canto II shares and manifests the process of "aging" as "The season changes." "Farewell to an idea," cantos II, III, and IV begin, reminding us that each section is a synecdoche of a mind ("idea") undergoing decreation. The mother of canto III is "dissolved" and "destroyed," while the house in which she lovingly resides with others is "half dissolved": "The house will crumble and the books will burn." The pathos of Stevens' wrenching sense of loss of home and mother is unmistakable in this canto, even though his own mother had died thirty-six years earlier. Stevens' loss of his parents, both as living and dead, will be examined in Chapter 4. I can think of no other example in Stevens where the sense of autumnal loss is more severe. The father of the succeeding canto is, in part, a foil to the mother by demonstrating that "The negations are never final," but, even so, like an enthroned Olympian deity, "He measures the velocities of change"; he does not arrest them. In canto VI a cosmic "theatre ... Collapsed," another image from the aurora borealis. The "named thing," whatever its costume and part, must be "nameless" and then "destroyed." A similar cosmic "imagination" is first pondered in questions and then realized in act in canto VII. It leaps among the heavens, "Extinguishing our planets, one by one" and leaving only a "shivering residue," like the surviving residue from "Autumn Refrain." Canto VIII conceives a final reductive point as "pure principle" and "innocence of the earth."

To render "The Auroras of Autumn" in this kind of rapid

survey is perhaps only to make another kind of paraphrase, but I wish to show that, in its barest manifestation, the poem is consistent and even redundant.

Canto VIII is the major canto of the poem and an important one in Stevens' canon. It posits the point toward which all the other reductions move, a point of innocence free of "false signs":

> For the oldest and coldest philosopher,
>
> There is or may be a time of innocence
> As pure principle ....
>
> It is like a thing of ether that exists
> Almost as predicate. But it exists,
> It exists, it is visible, it is, it is.
>
> So, then, these lights are not a spell of light,
> A saying out of a cloud, but innocence.
> An innocence of the earth and no false sign.

The aurora borealis overhead, like the stars in "The Reader" and "One of the Inhabitants of the West," leads him to "innocence of earth." "Innocence" is here akin to what he otherwise calls "ignorance," or knowledge of the earth without prejudice. Having three times said earlier "Farewell to an idea," he turns now to the earth's innocence as the alternative to those antiquaries. False ideas shunned, he can lay a claim on what in "Notes toward a Supreme Fiction" he calls "first idea." Such is the goal of all the poems of autumn, and the poet hopefully and intensely affirms its existence in staccato breathlessness ("But it exists, / It exists, it is visible, it is, it is.")

When one discovers the innocence of the earth, always temporarily and partially, self-reduction ends. Unhappy people in a happy world become happy people. "As the Angevine / Absorbs Anjou," in "A Dish of Peaches in Russia"; as "The man in Georgia waking among pines / Should be pine-spokesman," in "The Comedian as the Letter C," so the possessors of earth's innocence are "as Danes in Denmark all day long." As natives of their environment, impatient and distrustful of the "outlandish," they seem to come upon something like paradise. These have found, in canto IX, the "innocent earth" that was described in the preceding canto:

> We were as Danes in Denmark all day long
> And knew each other well, hale-hearted landsmen,
> For whom the outlandish was another day
>
> Of the week, queerer than Sunday. We thought alike
> And that made brothers of us in a home
> In which we fed on being brothers, fed
>
> And fattened as on a decorous honeycomb.
> This drama that we live.

And if Stevens' earthly paradise here seems overly masculine—it is, of course, only symbolically so—the forthcoming "rendezvous" with the world is feminine, "when she came alone." Outdistancing its autumnal setting for a moment, this canto suddenly breaks into summer, but this victory, like all of Stevens' victories, is short-lived: "Of what disaster is this the imminence: / Bare limbs, bare trees and a wind as sharp as salt?" the canto concludes. (It is worth noting that, when Stevens submitted to Alfred Knopf a list of poems that he wanted included in a never-published *Selected Poems*, he represented "The Auroras of Autumn" with these two cantos, VIII and IX.)[74]

Other respites assuage the harshness of decreation. As early as the first canto, for example, the poem speculates that the lights of the aurora may illumine the serpent, not as formlessness, but as master:

> These lights may finally attain a pole
> In the midmost midnight and find the serpent there,
>
> In another nest, the master of the maze
> Of body and air and forms and images,
> Relentlessly in possession of happiness.

If these lines anticipate briefly a "happiness" at the end of decreation, canto V seems to regress. The decreated father of canto IV relapses into the worst of his offenses. Now no longer in diminishment—or perhaps not yet so—both mother and father invite to their table a festival of "humanity." But the celebration of musicians, negresses, pageants, and herds succumbs to "insidious tones," and the guests are a "loud, disordered mooch" (V). In fact, the poem, which otherwise purges the loud discords of the imagination, here briefly allows them to run riot.

By progression and regression, the poem disallows a sense of direct development. Its dominant motif, however, is made up of tropes of decreation, like a fugue that recalls a central theme through variations and repetitions. As Donald Davie has observed, "The title prepares us: Aurora = dawn = beginning; Autumn = eve = ending. 'In my end is my beginning.' The cyclical pattern—this is the theme of the work."[75] It is another configuration of the end/beginning nexus that we have seen in many of the poems of autumn.[76]

The very trick in transforming unhappy people to happy people is to move from "extremity" to "Contriving balances." On such a note the poem concludes. "An unhappy people in a happy world" is our lot, but not permanently so. In meditating a whole, in balancing summer straw and winter's nick, one then enjoys—happily—the "pure principle" of the lights:

> Contriving balance to contrive a whole,
> The vital, the never-failing genius,
> Fulfilling his meditations, great and small.
>
> In these unhappy he meditates a whole,
> The full of fortune and the full of fate,
> As if he lived all lives, that he might know,
>
> In hall harridan, not hushful paradise,
> To a haggling of wind and weather, by these lights
> Like a blaze of summer straw, in winter's nick.
>
> (X)

71. Bloom, *Wallace Stevens: The Poems of Our Climate*, 254.

72. Joseph N. Riddel, *The Clairvoyant Eye: The Poetry and Poetics of Wallace Stevens* (Baton Rouge: Louisiana State University Press, 1965), 235.

73. Vendler, *On Extended Wings*, 250.

74. See George S. Lensing, *Wallace Stevens: A Poet's Growth* (Baton Rouge: Louisiana State University Press, 1986), 285.

75. Donald Davie, "The Auroras of Autumn," in *The Achievement of Wallace Stevens*, ed. Ashley Brown and Robert S. Haller (Philadelphia: J. B. Lippincott, 1962), 167.

76. The title had come from his notebook of titles, "From Pieces of Paper." See Lensing, *Wallace Stevens: A Poet's Growth*, 185.

—George S. Lensing. *Wallace Stevens and the Seasons*. Baton Rouge: Louisiana State University Press, 2001, pp. 96–100.

"The Course of a Particular"

"The Course of a Particular" appeared in the *Hudson Review* in 1950. However, despite that it appeared in print long before Knopf published *Collected Poems*, it was not collected there, nor was it added in any subsequent printings. Stevens claimed it was an oversight, but some critics—George S. Lensing (*q.v.*) being the most recent to say it—have expressed a suspicion that he withheld the poem on purpose. It stands to reason; Stevens was neither a disorganized nor a forgetful person, especially as his poetry was concerned.

Nearly every critic who has written about "The Course of a Particular" has noted the ideas and stylistic moves it shares with Stevens' earlier and more often anthologized poem, "The Snow Man." Both deal with a winter landscape, a particularity of perception, the role and task of the poet, and the uniquely "Stevens" definition of nothingness.

The title's abstract and theoretical sound is understandable if taken most literally: on one level of reading, the poem is about what happens to the specific. Considered in that light, and in the awareness of Stevens' ideas about the poetic necessity of the abstract, the poem's melancholy take on the fate of "the particular"—that is, the single, the specific, the concrete (the opposite of "nothing")—is not surprising.

"Today the leaves cry," opens the poem. The statement is, on the one hand, pathetic fallacy. However, without a solipsistic narration, the fallacy is not fulfilled. Instead, the poet's voice, nearly omniscient—"repressing" its ego, as one critic has termed it—moves into further consideration of the landscape while abstracting the personal stake in the moment. As a result, the poem does not descend to self-pitying woe on the part of its speaker. Rather, it continues to consider how "the nothingness of winter becomes a little less." Stevens' sense of what comprises "nothing" is outlined for the first time in "The Snow Man," where he wrote that it takes "a mind of winter" to see "beauty" in the harshness of the landscape, to "behold / Nothing that is not there, and the nothing that is." In other words, an eye with patience and the ability to see only what is revealed (the spare details, nothing more) as well as the nothingness, the negative space, that exists among such details. In the context of winter, a time of death to Stevens, as well as a time of solitude and reflection, the "nothing" becomes an undefined, a potential, and a void.

Expressed here, some three decades after he wrote "The Snow Man," the winter's nothingness "becomes a little less." In some sense, the winter is more jumbled, there is more to see, the leaves remain, as leaves on pin oaks and beeches do in the northeast. But "It is still full of icy shades and shapen snow." There is still contrast, more than simple death and stillness. The show, importantly, is shapen, which implies a hand in it, or the wind. The same wind sweeps the leaves.

As the leaves cry, "One holds off and merely hears the cry." As so often happens in Stevens, the pronoun is ambiguous, and deliberately so. It might be the universal pronoun for a person, as in "One must bathe daily." It might also refer directly to a leaf, acting as a third-person singular pronoun. The distinction is an important one. If Stevens were referring to a single leaf as standing off and listening to the cries of the others, the action would further the anthropomorphic gesture of the first line, and give more credence to the idea of a pathetic fallacy, thus undermining the omniscient voice of the poem. If, however, the reference is to the universal, the poem's narrative character is made more complex.

The cry is further described as a "busy cry, concerning someone else." The cry is characterized as distant from both the single leaf and the persona of the poem. The solitude of the listener approximates the role of the poet, in Stevens' evolving definition of the poet and poetry in other work to this point.

"And though one says that one is part of everything, // There is a conflict, there is a resistance involved; And being part is an exertion that declines: / One feels the life of that which gives life as it is." Here, the pronoun becomes clearer, diffusing some of the tension related to reference. It is clear that the one is meant to act as a universal particular, the one whose "course" is proscribed by the poem. The leaf, too, is a particular, and the relation between the speaker and the leaf is one of objective correlative, a rare move for Stevens (and a possible reason behind his reluctance to include the poem in *Collected Poems*). The stance of being apart, however, is clarified by the conflict. It is apparent to the speaker that he is part of everything, and yet there is a yearning to transcend. That is the conflict, the resistance. As one ages, the urge to be a part "declines" while at the same time one becomes more aware of the pervasive life—the nothing? The abstract and mysterious stuff of winter, that which is most clear when the landscape, when nature, is most still and reduced?— "which gives life as it is." In other words, a creator, a force of some sort, which makes life simply the way it is, not in any particular image.

Stevens then draws us again to the leaves and their cry. As if to build on the inherent creation alluded to in the previous line, he writes, "It is not a cry of divine attention," thus not a cry to a god or of a god. "Nor the smoked-drift of puffed-out heroes, nor human cry." In stating plainly what it is not, Stevens has restored the metaphor of the crying to its plain state. It is not human nor of the old heroes, therefore it is neither pathetic fallacy nor objective correlative. By calling such attention to the nature of his language, and by using so repetitious a strategy, Stevens works toward heightened and aware specificity. The definition of the cry becomes the drama of the poem, and is what moves it to its conclusion. By stripping away the artifice that could build around such a sensory and metaphorical appeal, through the use of rhetorical artifice, Stevens is working on both drive and precise abstraction at this point in the poem. He is a master working on our expectations and pushing them aside so that when we as readers reach the final stanzas, we, perhaps, see as clearly as he does.

"It is the cry of leaves that do not transcend themselves." The leaves are simply crying, not to anyone or about anything because, as he points out, they do not transcend. And it is becoming clear that the cry is not weeping or sobbing, but rather a shout, a yawp, something spoken. Whatever sadness overlays the poem is brought by the circumstances of winter, perhaps, if a reader is unfamiliar with Stevens and the fact that winter is seldom a source of sadness in his poems, and from the notions of crying and conflict. But the cry is clearly a message.

"In the absence of fantasia," there is no music, no accompaniment to the cries. With so much removed from our consideration, it almost becomes as though the cries are not even real. As such, the poem moves toward a similar conclusion: "without meaning more / Than they are in the final finding of the ear, in the thing / Itself, until, at last, the cry concerns no one at all." The final finding of the ear is simply sound, which could be as subtle as the leaves rubbing together. Beech leaves and oak leaves will make a whispering sound in winter, easily heard in the absence of everything else. In this way, perhaps Stevens' poem mimics the woods he spent a lifetime observing on his walks. When the cry is simply sound, simply "the thing itself," then it "concerns no one at all." It is enough that there is a cry. Or, because no one is concerned, it is simply the noise of leaves. In essence, Stevens is "de-creating," as Lensing puts it, or removing the accumulated meaning and getting back to "the thing itself." As the poem does this with the leaves, the ambiguity of its pronoun makes it clear that the poet is also in a stage of de-creating, in recognition of his increasing alienation and isolation.

"The Course of a Particular"

CHARLES BERGER ON NOTHINGNESS IN STEVENS

[In the excerpt, Berger discusses the idea of "nothing" in "The Course of a Particular," "The Snow Man," and other poems.]

Any reading of "The Course of a Particular" lives or dies on the poem's second line. "Yet the nothingness of winter becomes a little less" is as quietly outrageous a statement as Stevens ever made. How can nothingness become a little less? We make sense of the line only because "nothing" has a long history in Stevens; he has accustomed us to play with its meanings. If "the nothingness of winter becomes a little less," then it follows that the somethingness, or quiddity, of winter increases; or the special virtue of nothingness, its negative power, is on the wane. Of simple winter misery, there is no letup: "the leaves cry, hanging on branches swept by wind." In my discussion of "Esthétique du Mal," canto III, I pointed out the unsettling effect that the gallowslike image of hanging has on Stevens: it is indeed a sign of damnation. How does this sign accord with the lessening of winter's nothingness?

I think the key to this paradox lies in the poem to which "The Course of a Particular" responds, over a distance of more than thirty years. The crying of leaves in "The Snow Man" is borne by the sound of misery:

> misery in the sound of the wind,
> In the sound of a few leaves,
>
> Which is the sound of the land
> Full of the same wind
> That is blowing in the same bare place.

To become a snow man with a mind of winter, one must hold off and merely hear the sound of misery. But in the last stanza of "The Snow Man," the poet has become a "listener,"

who listens in the snow,
And, nothing himself, beholds
Nothing that is not there and the nothing that is.

By listening to the cry of the leaves, the cry of the land, Stevens was able "to behold"—the verb is as crucial as its objects—two versions of nothing. The first, "nothing that is not there," corresponds to "the absence of fantasia." But beyond or through that emerges a more powerful "nothing," a force defined positively as "the nothing that is." From this influx of negative energy flows the power to behold. Or, perhaps, the power to behold summons the discovery of "the nothing." In either case, that power comes from the trial of listening to the misery of the leaves without succumbing to pathos. "Behold" is a term we associate with prophetic contexts, and "The Snow Man" shows Stevens brought to the testing ground—the prophetic locus, the "same bare place"—in order to listen and to behold. The "wind" that blows through the land also blows through him, and the revelation of negativity is both won and bestowed, if only for the prophetic moment.

"The Course of a Particular" is a far quieter poem. No rushing wind, or spiritus, blows through the poem; mentioned in the opening line, "wind" (not *the* wind) stays there. The cry of the leaves, though heard throughout the poem, never rises in intensity. Whereas "The Snow Man" builds to power through the aggrandizement of repetition, coupled with the turning of short verses, the reiterations of "the leaves cry" does not magnify that irreducible sound, partly because of the poem's long, frequently end-stopped lines. Even the eye has dimmed somewhat: "icy shades and shapen snow" reports less than "pine-trees crusted with snow," "junipers shagged with ice," "spruces rough in the distant glitter." The effort to behold has turned into a holding off. And since so many of Stevens' late poems end with vocal epiphanies, the absence of voice here marks the poem's crisis as especially acute. "Esthétique du Mal," for example, ends with "the reverberating psalm, the right chorale"; "Auroras" closes with the rabbi's voice as he reads to the congregation; "The Owl in the Sarcophagus" gives us "a child that sings itself to sleep"; even "Ordinary Evening," in its final canto, explores sounds, words, speech, statement; and "The Rock" closes on "night's hymn of the rock." But in "The Course of a Particular," voice dwindles to cry and cry goes unanswered.

The poem's silence and the drift of its long lines reinforce the sense of entropy made explicit in "Being part [poet?] is an exertion that declines." More than the end of one poet is at stake here; the sequence, or line, that we call tradition seems to be petering out. One reason for the great power of "The Snow Man" has to do with Stevens' sense that he is standing in a line of seers; others have stood in that "same bare place." "The Course of a Particular" focuses on the other end of tradition, on the poet's legacy to those who come after. So Stevens at first asserts that "It is a busy cry, concerning someone else." Let the next in line attend to the cry. But by the end of the poem, "The cry concerns no one at all." Perhaps there *is* no successor.

What supplants the sustaining concept of tradition is the apprehension of a force behind life itself: "One feels the life of that which gives life as it is." In "Final Soliloquy of the Interior Paramour," a poem written at the same time as "The Course of a Particular," this mysterious "that"—perhaps we should call it "that which"—is sensed in the following way:

> We feel the obscurity of an order, a whole,
> A knowledge, that which arranged the rendezvous.

It seems as if the business of poetry, this late in Stevens' life and career, has become the feeling-out of the giver, or arranger. "Final Soliloquy" presents a more generous interpretation of this obscure spirit. The monosyllabic line from "The Course of a Particular" refuses to be inflected by feeling, but in moving beyond exertion to a giver of life on its own terms, Stevens seems to be approaching a threshold beyond which his own exertions, his poems, are no longer necessary. Moving beyond the "cry" into the region of "life as it is," Stevens puts exertion aside and allows himself to sense the given. "Life as it is," in this formulation, will resemble the region glimpsed in "Of Mere Being"—"Beyond the last thought ... on the edge of space."

—Charles Berger. *Forms of Farewell: The Late Poetry of Wallace Stevens*. Madison: The University of Wisconsin Press, 1985, pp. 158–161.

[Joseph Carroll is Professor of English at the University of Missouri at St. Louis. Carroll earned his Ph.D. at the University of California, Berkeley. He is the author of *The Cultural Theory of Matthew Arnold* (University of California Press, 1982); *Wallace Stevens' Supreme Fiction: A New Romanticism* (Louisiana State University Press, 1987); and *Evolution and Literary Theory* (University of Missouri Press, 1995). In a discussion on how the tenets of "Notes Toward a Supreme Fiction" work their way through Stevens' entire canon, Carroll points out how the poet and the leaves become unified in "The Course of a Particular."]

The supreme fiction effects an integration of the individual and the whole. In "The Course of a Particular" and "The Region November," Stevens depicts a state of being in which the integrative agency, the pure principle of sentient relation, has ceased to function. The particular to which Stevens refers in "The Course of a Particular" is at once himself and the phenomenon that absorbs his attention: the "cry" of the leaves on a winter day. The course of the poem is a meditation in which Stevens inverts the visionary process through which he comes to a realization of essential unity. As he listens to the sound of the leaves in the wind, he recedes into a state of alienation from the world around him:

> Today the leaves cry, hanging on branches swept by wind,
> Yet the nothingness of winter becomes a little less.
> It is still full of icy shades and shapen snow.
>
> The leaves cry ... One holds off and merely hears the cry.
> It is a busy cry, concerning someone else.
> And though one says that one is part of everything,
>
> There is a conflict, there is a resistance involved;
> And being part is an exertion that declines:
> One feels the life of that which gives life as it is. (*OP*, 96)

Stevens only gradually clarifies for himself the significance of the cry he hears. The declaration in the ninth line constitutes a climactic recognition. The force that "gives life as it is" is a force of particularity, that is, of "difference." In the first stanza, the cry of the leaves seems to associate itself with "the nothingness of winter" and also, paradoxically, to contribute to the diminution of spiritual negativity. The "icy shades and shapen snow" recall the landscape of "The Snow Man," a recollection that may help to account for the ambiguous mingling of nothingness and the incipient animism in the cry of the leaves. In the second stanza, perhaps because the nothingness of winter has become a little less, Stevens suggests that the cry is potentially meaningful, but only to "someone else," and his sense of alienation expands to include the social world. The declaration "being part is an exertion that declines" includes both the world of particular objects and the people who concern themselves with these objects.

Once he has clearly recognized "the life of that which gives life as it is," Stevens drives toward a complete inversion of the pure principle. He drains out the incipient animism in the leaves' cry, which, though it is a meaningless sound, echoes with the ironic pathos of spiritual absence:

> The leaves cry. It is not a cry of divine attention,
> Nor the smoke-drift of puffed-out heroes, nor human cry.
> It is the cry of leaves that do not transcend themselves,
>
> In the absence of fantasia, without meaning more
> Than they are in the final finding of the ear, in the thing
> Itself, until, at last, the cry concerns no one at all.

In Stevens' visionary poetry, man is an object of "divine attention" because he is the special locus of sentience through which the essential poem achieves its "difficult apperception" (*CP*, 440). The divine attention can be realized only through the forms of thought that are also the forms of phenomenal reality. These forms are the "fantasia" of the supreme fiction. The pure principle of sentient relation can articulate itself only in metaphoric displacements, "the intricate evasions of as" (*CP*,

486). The principle of difference manifests itself, here as in "Comedian," in a reduction to the literal, "life as it is." The forms of thought reduce themselves to "the final finding of the ear," and the forms of phenomenal reality reduce themselves to "the thing / Itself." In the absence of fantasia, these two aspects of particularity, the self and the world, are equivalent in their meaninglessness. Stevens repudiates essential unity, but he does not then revert to a celebration of the parts of the world. The failure of transcendental affect leaves him at the nadir of the cycle from Romanticism to indifferentism.

—Joseph Carroll. *Wallace Stevens' Supreme Fiction: A New Romanticism*. Baton Rouge: Louisiana State University Press, 1987, pp. 306–307.

DANIEL R. SCHWARZ ON THE CONFLICTS OF IMAGINATION

[In the excerpt, Schwarz contends that the poem illustrates the conflicting duty of artists—to both immerse themselves in the particulars of the world and maintain the separateness from them that is required for the creative imagination.]

We should imagine these later lyrics in a conversation with one another. Their subjects are the nature of poetry, the role of the creative imagination, and, of course, the feelings of the ageing Stevens about his art. We might think of the final lyrics as monologues spoken in scenes in a play. In 'The Course of a Particular' (1950), Stevens employs the tradition of *occupatio*, and creates meaning from the 'leaves cry', even as he claims to have resisted the 'exertion' to do so:

THE COURSE OF A PARTICULAR

Today the leaves cry, hanging on branches swept by wind,
Yet the nothingness of winter becomes a little less.
It is still full of icy shades and shapen snow.

The leaves cry ... One holds off and merely hears the cry.
It is a busy cry, concerning someone else.
And though one says that one is part of everything,

There is conflict, there is a resistance involved;
And being part is an exertion that declines:
One feels the life of that which gives life as it is.

The leaves cry. It is not a cry of divine attention,
Nor the smoke-drift of puffed-out heroes, nor human cry.
It is the cry of leaves that do not transcend themselves,

In the absence of fantasia, without meaning more
Than they are in the final finding of the ear, in the thing
Itself, until, at last, the cry concerns no one at all.

(PM, 367)

In 'The Course of a Particular', the poem immediately preceding 'Final Soliloquy of the Interior Paramour' in *The Palm at the End of the Mind*, the speaker grapples with his anxiety of ageing, his fatigue and his fear that his poetic powers are in decline. But in 'The Course of a Particular', he proposes the possibility of remaining in the nominalistic world and walking away from the strenuous and muscular effort required to write; as he writes in 'Long and Sluggish Lines' (1952), 'It makes so little difference, at so much more / Than seventy, here one looks, one has been there before.' The speaker stresses the element of choice; one can, he implies, 'hold off' and can refuse to accept the invitation of the objects of the world to have intercourse with them. Indeed, if he cannot control his imagination when he wishes, then the imagination's activity becomes a compulsion, something that holds one in its grip, even as it requires a terrifying effort in spite of one's desire to eschew involvement. Yet, while he says that he resists making the necessary effort—to domesticate the leaf in terms of his own experience—we see by the end of the poem that he has done so. Do we not feel that the dead leaves clinging to trees is a frightening image of obsolescence and mortality? If one metaphor defines the subject of the later lyrics, it is that one. Are not the leaves 'that do not transcend themselves' an image for Stevens's fear that he will not transcend his own particularity?

Perhaps the leaves recall the pages of a book—'the course of a particular'—and the material written on them; the cry of leaves is his poems asking hopefully, desperately, for a reading. While to be perceived as a particular thing is better than not being perceived at all, leaves are enriched by human perception—just as pages are given life by real readers reading. If the cry of leaves concerned 'no one at all', the poet would be locked in his own solipsistic world. In fact, as he narrates 'the course of the particular, he rescues it from particularity. For one thing, he not only directly refers to 'The Snow Man', where the ability to hear the sound of the wind is essential to overcome nothingness, but he actually replicates the poem in the first stanza where, for him, his perception of the sound of the wind blowing through leaves makes 'the nothingness of winter [become] a little less'.

'The Course of a Particular' enacts the conflicting tendency of the creative imagination—of all perceivers, including all readers—on the one hand, to make a commitment, to respond humanly, to engage oneself, and, on the other, to eschew involvement, to '[hold] off and merely [hear] the cry. In the later vein, one finds excuses for distancing events as if they were of no moral or emotional concern, as if they were the business of 'someone else'. Isn't the impersonal pronoun 'one' a way of distancing the emotion of 'I', a way of avoiding the very quest for meaning that the writing of the poem proves as having taken place? With its absence of a first-person narrator, this poem tests the idea that lyrics might be other than a drama of consciousness only to discard the idea as fallacious. Does not the thrice-repeated 'cry of leaves' transform the poem into a chant giving praise to the leaves, even as they conclude their course in the punning finale in which Stevens stresses the homophonic relationship between 'ear' and 'air'—'the final finding of the [poet's] air?' The iteration of 'cry'—which is 'not a cry of divine attention'—as a sound external to the perceiver, underlines how the self-conscious speaker is wrenched from brooding on his decline. Yet he inserts the generic story of life from the original baby's cry to the feared lonely 'cry' of his (and our) final end. Isn't the tale of 'conflict' and 'resistance'—of 'puffed-out heroes' ending in 'smoke-drift' and 'decline'—a submerged biography, a course of a particular, as surely as Cummings's narrative, 'anyone lived in a little how town'?

—Daniel R. Schwarz. *Narrative and Representation in the Poetry of Wallace Stevens.* New York: St. Martin's Press, 1993, pp. 209–211.

George S. Lensing on the Poem's Relation to "The Snow Man"

[In the excerpt, Lensing describes the "dialogue" between the poem and "The Snow Man."]

When Stevens wrote "The Snow Man" in 1921 he must have fully appreciated its success as a lyric as well as its importance to his own poetics. In the many poems of winter that he would write over the succeeding decades, they all have a certain genesis in "The Snow Man" and receive a frame of reference from it. It is as if Stevens wanted to explain this *ur*-poem by rewriting it over and over. I want to examine that rewriting in terms of the way each poem impresses upon us Stevens' powerful need to know and unite with a world in which he might confidently believe. "I must impale myself on reality," he wrote toward the end of his life in a note for an unwritten poem (*OP* [Morse], xxiv).

In four poems, "The Course of a Particular," "In a Bad Time," "Man Carrying Thing," and "Vacancy in the Park," Stevens repeats the kind of extreme decreation that he poses in "The Snow Man." I can think of few poets, the Christian mystics of the dark night of the soul being a possible exception, who more ruthlessly and radically restrain the ego, even to the limits of consciousness itself. That scheme becomes programmatic in poems of winter like these. In "The Snow Man" we have seen one example of such reduction, but how could Stevens, in subsequent poems, continue to convey a poetry of radical absence and abnegation?

Almost exactly forty years after "The Snow Man," Stevens wrote "The Course of a Particular" (*OP* 123–24). It appeared in the *Hudson Review* in 1951 but was not included in *Collected Poems* three years later. When Robert Pack wrote asking about the omission, Stevens replied that he didn't even know that he left it out and that this and any other omissions resulted "because I had not kept a copy of the manuscript or had misplaced it" (*L* 881). There is, it seems to me, something disingenuous in this excuse. Stevens was not one to "withdraw" poems in the manner of Auden, for example, but he did from time to time leave aside poems that seemed to him inadequate. In the case of "The Course of a Particular" the issue could not have been inadequacy. It seems to me to belong with "The Plain Sense of Things," "To an Old Philosopher in Rome," "The World as Meditation," "The River of Rivers in Connecticut," "Prologues to What Is Possible," "Final Soliloquy of the Interior Paramour," and others as among his great poems of advanced age. With his usual penchant for *kerygma*, Yvor Winters calls "The Course of a Particular" "one of the greatest poems in English."[40] My own theory is that Stevens may have feared that the poem was too obviously a rewriting of "The Snow Man" and that it might easily—perhaps too easily—be seen as such. I might add that placing the two poems side by side, separated otherwise by four decades, one notes how little certain aspects of Stevens' style actually changed over the years. As a poet not given to repeating himself, especially a poet who was seventy-three years old, he may simply have wanted to protect himself from such a charge and elected to leave it out of the *Collected Poems*. In spite of the praise of Winters and others, it has tended to be neglected by Stevens' readers and, while it is not as great a poem as "The Snow Man," it belongs in the front ranks of his works.

Both poems are fifteen lines in tercets describing the evolution of "one" to "no one." Both expel "fantasia" from a scene of merciless winter severity. The cry of leaves in "The Course of a Particular" echoes the "sound of a few leaves" in "The Snow Man" and the turning leaves in "Domination of Black." Once again, "the nothingness of winter" is imposed. The poem begins:

> Today the leaves cry, hanging on branches swept by wind,
> Yet the nothingness of winter becomes a little less.
> It is still full of icy shades and shapen snow.

The nothingness of winter is lessened only momentarily: a

human ear is clearly present at the outset to perceive the cry ("One holds off and merely hears the cry"). The poem's movement, nonetheless, is in the other direction: from the lessening of winter to its intensification, from a perceived something to unperceived nothing, from the presence of the self in conjunction with the world toward severance from it. Unlike "The Snow Man," this poem does not lay out wintry beauty and austere pleasure. "Icy shades and shapen snow" remain merely abstract. Only the plaintive cry of the leaves is heard.

> And though one says that one is part of everything,
>
> There is a conflict, there is a resistance involved;
> And being part is an exertion that declines.

That conflict and resistance now dissociate the beholder from the scene and deny him a part in it. The progress of that "decline" is the "course" of Stevens' particular world and this particular poem—the widening distance between the human ear and the leaves' cry. It is first reported as "a busy cry, concerning someone else," but even the someone else is abruptly dismissed:

> The leaves cry. It is not a cry of divine attention,
> Nor the smoke-drift of puffed-out heroes, nor human cry.
> It is the cry of leaves that do not transcend themselves,
>
> In the absence of fantasia, without meaning more
> Than they are in the final finding of the ear, 41 in the thing
> Itself, until, at last, the cry concerns no one at all.

The speaker refuses to bestow any signification upon the cry. There is no divine instress to be "Spelt from Sibyl's Leaves," as in Hopkins' poem. The cry of these leaves conjures no human heroism nor human of any kind. "Without meaning more / Than they are," the leaves are a "final finding" of the ear, like the "final refuge" of "Autumn Refrain." But even the "final finding" is merely almost final until the lingering ear is itself effaced in the last line: "until, at last, the cry concerns no one at all."

Stevens' choice of the word "cry" to describe the leaves implies a strong invitation to pathetic fallacy, a fantasia he resists, but whose lure is powerful. (A similar use of the word occurs in the "cry" of the sea in "The Idea of Order at Key West.") The poet fights off those Aeolian sirens of his Romantic predecessors: Shelley in "Ode to the West Wind" ("Make me thy lyre, even as the forest is: / What if my leaves are falling like its own!")[42] and Coleridge in "Dejection: An Ode" ("I turn from you, and listen to the wind, / Which long has raved unnoticed. What a scream / Of agony by torture lengthened out / That lute sent forth!").[43]

The "final finding of the ear" here yields a different satisfaction, "the thing / Itself," the goal of every winter peregrination. The total possession of the thing, as we have seen in "The Snow Man," exacts the cancellation of the self as a separate entity, a daunting and devastating price. But that is precisely what "The Course of a Particular" itself proposes in the final line. The three commas stretch out the temporal span ("Itself, until, at last ..."), as the poem's earlier Alexandrines expand into two final heptameters, coming to rest finally in the same "nothing" of "The Snow Man." The poem, in fact, has moved from the cry heard by "One" but "concerning someone else" to the conclusion where it "concerns no one at all." Nor is there anything of a transcendent "divine attention" in the cry, nor a cry of "puffed-out heroes, nor human cry." But through its denials, the poem arrives at affirmation. The leaves' cry transcends nothing "without meaning more / Than they are." The course of the particular is to arrive at the pure affirmation of "are," even if "are" is first the discovery of "ear," but finally that of "no one."

Many of Stevens critics, from Yvor Winters to Harold Bloom, note intimations of death in the poem's finale. So radical a reduction of the self can hardly seem otherwise, just as in "The Snow Man." Stevens' self-cancellation, however, is epistemological rather than homicidal; the final "absence of fantasia" can be attained only by an absence of the perceiving self. As William W. Bevis has noted, "He has progressed in the poem beyond thought ('says'), beyond imagination ('fantasia'), and beyond feeling ('concern'), to some ultimate perception, a 'final finding of the ear,' which 'at last' issues in negation: 'no one at all.'"[44]

"The Snow Man" remakes "One" into the human nothingness

of a snow man; "The Course of a Particular" ends with simple absence. The "thing / Itself," is unmediated *Ding an sich* and preserved as such by the dismissal of its translator. But by the poem's variously imposed absences, it has gained its particular. Its "nothingness of winter" is, as in "The Snow Man," a "nothing that is."

NOTES

40. Yvor Winters, "Wallace Stevens, or the Hedonist's Progress," in *On Modern Poets* (New York: Meriden Books, 1959), 35.

41. Milton Bates, in his edition of *Opus Posthumous*, removes the misprinted "air" of the first edition of that work and reinserts "ear" in the second-last line.

42. *The Complete Works of Percy Bysshe Shelley*, ed. Roger Ingpen and Walter E. Peck (New York: Gordian Press, 1965), 2:297.

43. *Coleridge: Selected Poems*, ed. Richard Holmes (London: Harper Collins, 1996), 182.

44. William W. Bevis, *Mind of Winter: Wallace Stevens, Meditation, and Literature* (Pittsburgh: University of Pittsburgh Press, 1989), 55.

—George S. Lensing. *Wallace Stevens and the Seasons.* Baton Rouge: Louisiana State University Press, 2001, pp.144–147.

WORKS BY

Wallace Stevens

Harmonium, 1923.

Ideas of Order, 1935.

Owl's Clover, 1936.

The Man with the Blue Guitar, and Other Poems, 1937.

Parts of a World, 1942.

Notes Toward a Supreme Fiction, 1942.

Esthetique du Mal, 1945.

Transport to Summer, 1947.

Three Academic Pieces: The Realm of Resemblance, Someone Puts a Pineapple Together, Of Ideal Time and Choice, 1947.

A Primitive Like an Orb, 1948.

The Auroras of Autumn, 1950.

The Relations between Poetry and Painting, 1951.

Selected Poems, 1952.

Selected Poems, 1953.

Raoul Duly: A Note, 1953.

The Collected Poems of Wallace Stevens, 1954.

Opus Posthumous, (edited by Samuel French Morse), 1957.

Poems by Wallace Stevens (edited by Samuel French Morse), 1959.

The Necessary Angel: Essays on Reality and the Imagination, 1960.

Letters of Wallace Stevens (edited by Holly Stevens), 1966.

The Palm at the End of the Mind: Selected Poems and a Play by Wallace Stevens (edited by Holly Stevens), 1971.

Collected Poetry and Prose, 1997.

Wallace Stevens

Arensberg, Mary, ed. *The American Sublime*. Albany: State University of New York Press, 1986.

Bahti, Timothy. "End and Ending: On the Lyric Technique of Some Wallace Stevens Poems." *MLN* 105 (December 1990): pp. 1046–62.

Baker, Peter. "Languages of Modern Poetry." *College Literature* 21 (June 1994): pp. 151–55.

Barnard, Rita. "'The Bread of Faithful Speech': Wallace Stevens, Ideology, and War." *Essays in Literature* 17 (Spring 1990): pp. 69–75.

Bates, Milton J. "Wallace Stevens' Final Yes: A Response to Sister Bernetta Quinn." *Renascence* 41 (Summer 1989): pp. 205–8.

———. *Wallace Stevens: A Mythology of Self*. Berkeley: University of California Press, 1985.

Bauer, Paul. "The Politics of Reticence: Wallace Stevens in the Cold War Era." *Twentieth Century Literature* 39 (Spring 1993): pp. 1–31.

Beehler, Michael. *T.S. Eliot, Wallace Stevens, and the Discourses of Difference*. Baton Rouge: Louisiana State University Press, 1987.

Bloom, Harold. *Wallace Stevens: The Poems of Our Climate*. Ithaca, NY: Cornell University Press, 1977.

Bloom, Harold, ed. *Wallace Stevens*. New York: Chelsea House, 1984.

Booker, M. Keith. "Notes Toward a Lacanian Reading of Wallace Stevens." *Journal of Modern Literature* 16 (Spring 1990): pp. 493–509.

Brogan, Jacqueline Vaught. "Wallace Stevens: 'The Sound of Right Joining.'" *Studies in Literature and Language* 28 (Spring 1986): pp. 107–20.

Buchsbaum, Betty. "Contours of Desire: The Place of Cezanne in Wallace Stevens' Poetics and Late Practice." *Criticism* 30 (Summer 1988): pp. 303–24.

Byers, Thomas B. *What I Cannot Say: Self, Word, and World in Whitman, Stevens, and Merwin*. Urbana: University of Illinois Press, 1989.

Castellito, George P. "A Taste of Fruit: The Extended Hand in William Carlos Williams and Imaginative Distance in Wallace Stevens." *Papers on Language & Literature* 28 (Fall 1992): pp. 442–50.

———. "Paradise in Wallace Stevens' 'Sunday Morning' and 'Esthétique du Mal.'" *CLA Journal* 33 (March 1990): pp. 298–307.

Chabot, C. Barry. *Writers for the Nation: American Literary Modernism.* Tuscaloosa: University of Alabama Press, 1997.

Cleghorn, Angus J. *Wallace Stevens' Poetics: The Neglected Rhetoric.* New York: Palgrave, 2000.

Cook, Albert. "The French Mutations of Wallace Stevens." *Journal of Modern Literature* 22:1 (Fall 1998): pp. 93–115.

Cook, Eleanor. "Wallace Stevens and the King James Bible." *Essays in Criticism* 41 (July 1991): pp. 240–52.

———. *Poetry, Word-Play, and Word-War in Wallace Stevens.* Princeton: Princeton University Press, 1988.

Costello, Bonnie. "'What to Make of a Diminished Thing': Modern Nature and Poetic Response." *American Literary History* 10:4 (Winter 1998): pp. 569-605.

Crowder, A.B. *Poets and Critics: Their Means and Meanings: Including Essays on Browning, Ruskin, Stevens, Heaney, and Others.* Lewiston: Edwin Mellen Press, 1993.

Dickie, Margaret. *Lyric Contingencies: Emily Dickinson and Wallace Stevens.* Philadelphia: University of Pennsylvania Press, 1991.

Doreski, William. "Wallace Stevens in Connecticut." *Twentieth Century Literature* 39 (Summer 1993): pp. 152–65.

Doud, Robert E. "The Trinity After Breakfast: Theology and Imagination in Wallace Stevens and Alfred North Whitehead." *Journal of the American Academy of Religion* 52 (September 1984): pp. 481–98.

Doyle, Charles, ed. *Wallace Stevens: The Critical Heritage.* Boston: Routledge & K. Paul, 1985.

Estrin, Barbara L. "Space-Off and Voice-Over: Adrienne Rich and Wallace Stevens." *Women's Studies* 25:1 (1995): pp. 23–46.

Feshbach, Sidney. "A Pretext for Wallace Stevens' 'Sunday Morning.'" *Journal of Modern Literature* 23: 1 (Summer 1999): p. 59–78.

Filreis, Alan. *Modernism from Right to Left: Wallace Stevens, the Thirties, & Literary Radicalism*. New York: Cambridge University Press, 1994.

———. *Wallace Stevens and the Actual World*. Princeton: Princeton University Press, 1991.

———. "Wallace Stevens and the Strength of the Harvard Reaction." *The New England Quarterly* 58 (March 1985): pp. 27–45.

———. "Wallace Stevens and the Crisis of Authority." *American Literature* 56 (December 1984): pp. 560–78.

Fischer, John. "Wallace Stevens and the Idea of a Central Poetry." *Criticism* 26 (Summer 1984): pp. 259–72.

Fisher, Barbara. *Wallace Stevens: The Intensest Rendezvous*. Charlottesville: University Press of Virginia, 1990.

Gardner, James. "Professor Vendler's Garden of Verses." *Commentary* 81 (January 1986) pp. 50–5.

Gelpi, Albert, ed. *Wallace Stevens: The Poetics of Modernism*. New York: Cambridge University Press, 1985.

Green, Thomas M. "Poetry and Permeability." *New Literary History* 30:1 (Winter 1999): pp. 75–91.

Grey, Thomas C. *The Wallace Stevens Case: Law and the Practice of Poetry*. Cambridge: Harvard University Press, 1991.

Halliday, Mark. *Stevens and the Interpersonal*. Princeton: Princeton University Press, 1991.

Harrington, Joseph. "Wallace Stevens and the Poetics of National Insurance." *American Literature* 67 (March 1995): pp. 95–114.

Helsa, David H. "Singing in Chaos: Wallace Stevens and Three or Four Ideas." *American Literature* 57 (May 1985): pp. 240–62.

Henry, Parrish Dice. "In the Connecticut Grain: The Final World of Wallace Stevens." *The Kenyon Review* 7 (Winter 1985): pp. 85–91.

Hertz, David Michael. *Angels of Reality: Emersonian Unfoldings in Wright, Stevens, and Ives*. Carbondale: Southern Illinois University Press, 1993.

Hoagland, Tony. "On Disproportion." *Parnassus: Poetry in Review* 19:2 (1994): pp. 110–27.

Jarraway, David R. "'Creatures of the Rainbow': Wallace Stevens, Mark Doty, and the Poetics of Androgyny." *Mosaic* 30 (September 1997): pp. 169–83.

———. *Wallace Stevens and the Question of Belief: Metaphysician in the Dark*. Baton Rouge: Louisiana State University Press, 1993.

Jenkins, Lee M. *Wallace Stevens: Rage for Order*. Brighton: Sussex Academic Press, 2000.

Lakritz, Andrew M. *Modernism and the Other in Stevens, Frost, and Moore*. Gainesville: University Press of Florida, 1996.

Leggett, B.J. *Wallace Stevens and Poetic Theory: Conceiving the Supreme Fiction*. Chapel Hill: University of North Carolina Press, 1987.

Lensing, George S. *Wallace Stevens: A Poet's Growth*. Baton Rouge: Louisiana State University Press, 1986.

Lentricchia, Frank. *Ariel and the Police: Michel Foucault, William James, Wallace Stevens*. Madison: University of Wisconsin Press, 1988.

———. "Patriarchy Against Itself: The Young Manhood of Wallace Stevens." *Critical Inquiry* 13 (Summer 1987) pp. 742–86.

Leonard, James S. and C.E. Wharton. "Wallace Stevens as Phenomenologist." *Texas Studies in Literature and Language* 26 (Fall 1984): pp. 331–61.

Lombardi, Thomas F. *Wallace Stevens and the Pennsylvania Keystone: The Influence of Origins on His Life and Poetry*. Selinsgrove: Susquehanna University Press, 1996.

Longenbach, James. *Wallace Stevens: The Plain Sense of Things*. New York: Oxford University Press, 1991.

MacLeod, Glen G. *Wallace Stevens and Modern Art: From the Armory Show to Abstract Expressionism*. New Haven: Yale University Press, 1993.

Mao, Douglas. "Wallace Stevens for the Millennium: The Spectacle of Enjoyment." *Southwest Review* 85:1 (2000): pp. 10–33.

McCann, Janet. *Wallace Stevens Revisited: "The Celestial Possible."* New York: Twayne Publishers, 1995.

Murphy, Charles M. *Wallace Stevens: A Spiritual Poet in a Secular Age*. New York: Paulist Press, 1997.

Newcomb, John Timberman. *Wallace Stevens and Literary Canons.* Jackson: University Press of Mississippi, 1992.

———. "Others, Poetry, and Wallace Stevens: Little Magazines as Agents of Reputation." *Essays in Literature* 16 (Fall 1989): pp. 256–70

Penso Kia. *Wallace Stevens, Harmonium, and the Whole of Harmonium.* Hamden: Archon Books, 1991.

Perricone, Christopher. "Poetic Philosophy: The Wittgenstein–Stevens Connection." *Philosophy Today* 44:3 (Fall 2000): pp. 245–58.

Pfau, Thomas. "Confluences: Reading Wallace Stevens." *Southwest Review* 84: 4 (1999) pp. 601–15.

Powell, Grosvenor. "Sturge Moore's *The Powers of the Air*: Socrates and the Self-Regarding Figure of Wallace Stevens." *The Modern Language Review* 88 (April 1993): pp. 283–96.

Quinn, Bernetta. "Wallace Stevens: 'The Peace of the Last Intelligence.'" *Renascence* 41 (Summer 1989): pp. 191–210.

Rieke, Alison. *The Senses of Nonsense.* Iowa City: University of Iowa Press, 1992.

Rosu, Anca. *The Metaphysics of Sound in Wallace Stevens.* Tuscaloosa: University of Alabama Press, 1995.

Sampson, Theodore. *A Cure of the Mind: The Poetics of Wallace Stevens.* Montreal: Black Rose Books, 2000.

Samuels, Lisa and Jerome J. McGann. "Deformance and Interpretation." *New Literary History* 30:1 (Winter 1999): pp. 25–56.

Schaum, Melita, ed. *Wallace Stevens and the Feminine.* Tuscaloosa: University of Alabama Press, 1993.

———. *Wallace Stevens and the Critical Schools.* Tuscaloosa: University of Alabama Press, 1988.

Schleifer, Ronald and Nancy M. West. "The Poetry of What Lies Close at Hand: Photography, Commodities, and Postromantic Discourses in Hardy and Stevens." *Modern Language Quarterly* 60:1 (March 1999): pp. 33–57.

Schoening, Mark. "Sacrifice and Sociability in the Modern Imagination: Wallace Stevens and the Cold War." *Contemporary Literature* 41:1 (Spring 2000): pp. 138–61.

Schulze, Robin G. *The Web of Friendship: Marianne Moore and Wallace Stevens*. Ann Arbor: The University of Michigan Press, 1995.

Sharpe, Tony. *Wallace Stevens: A Literary Life*. New York: St. Martin's Press, 2000.

Smith, Evans Lansing. "The Lyrical Nekyia: Metaphors of Poesis in Wallace Stevens." *Journal of Modern Literature* 21:2 (Winter 1997-1998): pp. 201–8.

Sperry, Stuart M. "Wallace Stevens and Poetic Transformation." *Raritan* 17 (Winter 1998): pp. 25–46.

———. "Wallace Stevens and the Seasons." *The Southern Review* 33 (Summer 1997): pp. 605–27.

Steinman, Lisa Malinowki. *Made in America: Science, Technology, and American Modernist Poets*. New Haven: Yale University Press, 1987.

Vendler, Helen. *Wallace Stevens: Words Chosen Out of Desire*. Knoxville: University of Tennessee Press, 1984.

Voros, Gyorgi. *Notations of the Wild: Ecology in the Poetry of Wallace Stevens*. Iowa City: University of Iowa Press, 1997.

Wyatt, David. "Working the Field." *The Southern Review* 36:4 (Autumn 2000): pp. 874–80.

ACKNOWLEDGMENTS

"Wallace Stevens" by J. Hillis Miller. From *Critical Essays on Wallace Stevens*, eds. Steven Gould Axelrod and Helen Deese. Boston: G.K. Hall & Co., 1988: 81–83. © 1988 by G.K. Hall & Co. Reprinted by permission of The Gale Group.

The Poetry of Wallace Stevens by Robert Rehder. London: The MacMillan Press Ltd., 1988: 65-69, 142–144. © 1988 by The MacMillan Press Ltd. Reprinted by permission.

Reading and Writing Nature by Guy Rotella. Boston: Northeastern University Press, 1991: 114–116, 119–122. © 1991 by Northeastern University Press. Reprinted by permission.

Early Stevens: The Nietzschean Intertext by B.J. Leggett. Durham: Duke University Press, 1992: 119–122, 185–186, 205. © 1992 by Duke University Press. Reprinted by permission.

Modernist Quartet by Frank Lentricchia. New York: Cambridge University Press, 1994: 131–136. © 1994 by Cambridge University Press. Reprinted with the permission of Cambridge University Press.

Wallace Stevens' Experimental Language: The Lion in the Lute by Beverly Maeder. New York: St. Martin's Press, 1999: 19–23. © 1999 by Beverly Maeder. Reprinted with permission of Palgrave Macmillan.

Mind of Winter: Wallace Stevens, Meditation, and Literature by William W. Bevis. Pittsburgh: University of Pittsburgh Press, 1988: 147–149, 255–260. © 1988 by The University of Pittsburgh Press. Reprinted by permission of the Univeristy of Pittsburgh Press.

The Fluent Mundo: Wallace Stevens and the Structure of Reality by J.S. Leonard and C.E. Wharton. Athens: The University of Georgia Press, 1988: 33–35, 43–44. © 1988 by The University of Georgia Press. Reprinted by permission.

INDEX OF
Themes and Ideas